Weep Not Fo...

To Rashid, Sir Sidney Hamburger,
and all who strive for peace

Weep Not For Me

Geoffrey Howard

Foreword by David Sheppard

DARTON · LONGMAN + TODD

First published in 1993 by
Darton, Longman and Todd Ltd
1 Spencer Court
140–142 Wandsworth High Street
London SW18 4JJ

ISBN 0–232–52041–0

A catalogue record for this book is available
from the British Library

Scripture quotations are taken from the
New Jerusalem Bible, published and copyright 1985
by Darton, Longman and Todd Ltd and Doubleday & Co Inc.
and used by permission of the publishers

Phototypeset by Intype, London
Printed and bound in Great Britain at
The University Press, Cambridge

Contents

Preface

Little is known about the walk of Jesus from the Antonia fortress to Golgotha. We know that Simon of Cyrene helped carry the cross and that Jesus spoke to the women of Jerusalem. It is not known if Jesus met his mother, nor if he fell, nor if Veronica mopped his face with a towel. Whether or not the acts which we mark as Stations of the Cross are fact or myth, they are a powerful comment on the human condition.

In these meditations, I have woven scripture, tradition, conjecture and contemporary experience to make a Via Dolorosa down which I invite you to walk. It is not an easy road and I promise little comfort.

I am grateful for those who have allowed me to use their stories. In some cases, I have, at their request, changed their names and unimportant details. One such person is Rashid, to whom, with others, I have dedicated this book. For his own safety, his real name and identity have been preserved.

Foreword

How we view the events of today's world is often decisively influenced by which side of the tracks we see them from. That is also true of how we see the Stations of the Cross.

Our desire for a neat and tidy system of faith encourages us to ignore the viewpoints of many groups, whose hurtful experiences on the wrong side of the tracks block the uncomplicated view which some of us may have.

Geoffrey Howard will not allow us to limit our viewing platform to comfortable Christian ground. In *Weep Not For Me* we find ourselves surrounded by emaciated hands held out for food: we stand in the shoes of a Muslim teenager and of a Jewish businessman in Manchester. The scarlet thread running down the middle of these painful human experiences is the story of the last week of Jesus' life, condemned to death, carrying his cross. Down the centuries this part of the gospels, probably the first section to be committed to writing, has inspired millions who suffer to believe there is a God who understands.

We long to make sense of this world and for its different lines to be seen to converge. Geoffrey Howard takes us to places where, the more we know, the more it seems that the lines of human experience and understanding grow further apart. We hear divergent voices, who describe the same Holy Land in utterly different ways: for example, a Jewish soldier, recently arrived from Ethiopia, speaks of Israel's perils, surrounded by many enemies. Palestinians protest that their homes have been taken away and that opportunities are unjustly denied to their young people.

This chairman of the North-West Friends of Israel insists that he must speak up about the injustices he sees

Palestinians facing. He expects he will be asked to resign his chairmanship, but his Jewish friend does not want him to resign.

Nails are still being hammered into Jesus' hands and feet in our world. Yet these painful glimpses of today's realities provide fresh insights into the Stations of the Cross. We are consistently brought back to the Lord who enters into our suffering: we want him to be strong, to bounce back, to take control again. We are confused when he is weak and vulnerable.

There is a 'not yet' about Holy Week – the Lord not yet bringing all things into subjection under his feet. What we do see there is enduring love, not offering neat solutions, but staying with our messy, unresolved, human situations – always with the promise of resurrection ahead of us. From these uneven platforms this Lent book offers us fresh insight into who Jesus is.

+ David Liverpool

Liverpool, August 1993

Introduction: Flight to the Cross

It is Monday 22 February 1992, my forty-eighth birthday. I am bound for Tel Aviv on El Al flight 312, 38,000 feet above Southern Germany. I have just finished eating a chicken dinner and have leaned back with my notebook and pencil, sipping occasionally from my second glass of red wine. I should be contented, but I am filled with dread. On Friday, I will join the Franciscans as they follow the Stations of the Cross along the Via Dolorosa. Though this is my primary reason for visiting Israel, there is another item on the agenda. I have a Via Dolorosa of my own to walk. I am about to take steps that could tear my emotions and my loyalties apart.

In recent years, I have helped to build bridges between the Christian and Jewish communities in England. The British National Party has rained insults on the local Jews. Supporters of the BNP have issued threats. In their underground newspapers and in secret meetings, they have claimed that while the Holocaust was a hoax, they will get it right next time. In the press, in worship and at public gatherings I have spoken out against this evil. Consequently, I have developed deep friendships with people within the Jewish community.

Four years ago, as a gesture of friendship to that community, I accepted the chairmanship of the North-West Friends of Israel Association. I did not take this on lightly. Before agreeing, I was assured that the organisation was non-political. I would be chairing meetings on subjects such as the botany and ornithology of Israel. This has been the case and I have never been overtly compromised. However, as I have learnt more about the Palestinian situation, the chair has become increasingly more uncomfortable. I might console myself by saying that the Friends of Israel Association is non-political, but I cannot deny that its name conveys my support for a regime which some believe to be responsible for certain injustices.

Although the organisation is purely cultural, it would be embarrassing if the chairman, even in his private capacity, were to make statements about the injustice of the Palestinian situation. Furthermore, for some of my Jewish friends, the words Jewish and Zionist are synonymous. In their minds, to speak out against injustice in Israel is to be anti-Semitic. My problem is compounded by the fact that I know of the Palestinian situation only through the media. If I voiced my anxieties, they would be soothed away by people who know the situation first hand. Thus I am gagged.

Were I to believe that the current talks between the Israelis and the Palestine Liberation Organisation would bear fruit, I might have an easier mind, hoping that the hands that pull me apart might soon be joined. I have no optimism. To many Israelis, the Palestinians are the Philistines with whom they have been in conflict since early biblical times. To the Palestinians, the Israelis are westerners who have stolen their land.

So I am off to Israel, not just to join with the Franciscans as they follow the Stations of the Cross, but to find out for myself about Israel and its relations with Palestinians. My prayer is that this trip will also be an inspiration for the meditations that follow.

My intention in this book is not to focus primarily on this trip. This 'mission' will be a catalyst, helping me to see the Stations in situations at home and in events in other parts of the world.

As the Boeing 737 roars over the snow caps of the Austrian Alps, I put the glass of wine to my lips once more. It may be my last cup of comfort for some time.

1 Jesus is Condemned to Death

'If you set him free you are no friend of Caesar's; anyone who makes himself king is defying Caesar.' Hearing these words, Pilate had Jesus brought out, and seated him on the chair of judgement at a place called the Pavement, in Hebrew Gabbatha.

(John 19:12–13)

It is 30 January 1975. I am camping in a one-man tent. It is too windy outside to cook, so I take the stove under cover.

I am lying down the length of my tent, with my head at the blind end and my feet near the zipped-up flaps. I am writing by candlelight while my meat pudding is steaming. It should have taken 25 minutes, but I am so absorbed that after three-quarters of an hour, I notice that the stove has long since gone out and the meat pudding is cold. The gas cylinder is empty. Hunger and the thought of waiting another 25 minutes exasperate me. Annoyed and impatient, I take a new cylinder and begin to fit it, although normally, I change cylinders outside. Before the operation is complete, there is a leak of gas. Butane is being sprayed up my arm and into my face. Instantly, it ignites on the candle and I am a ball of flame. With an explosion of adrenalin, I throw myself blindly to the other end of the tent. I can neither see nor breathe. My eyelids are shutting out the heat and my lungs refuse to inhale the fire that is raging around me. I am fully clothed and wearing a hat but my hands and face feel as if they are in scalding water.

I am fighting to open the zips but they are melting.

Consciousness is slipping away. My mind is being propelled from my body towards a cinema screen on which a picture of my wife and children is projected. I am flying through the air towards the ever enlarging look of horror on their faces as they witness my death.

The horizontal zip gives in my hands and my mind is brought back into the inferno. A strength greater than my own takes over and I become an enraged animal clawing for my life. My hands and face are aflame, while through tightly closed eyes I see brightness like the sun. The vertical zip gives and my head is rammed through the gap, gasping cold air. I burst out into the night as orange flames crackle three metres into the night sky. So ends the longest three seconds of my life. I put out my smouldering clothing and examine the blisters on my hands and face.

While I was engulfed in flame, I thought I was dying. But now that I am out of the blaze with no more than minor burns, the death sentence still seems to hang over me. It has not been lifted, but postponed. Having looked death in the face, I can never again avert its gaze. I have cheated it, but I cannot cheat it forever. Whether the executioner comes today or in 20 years, he will come. It is as if I am in a cell waiting for him. There is no escape. Neither tears, contrition, piety nor energy can commute this sentence. Like a man who petitions a court of appeal, I might through careful diet and medical care postpone the day. But eventually I will hear the key in the lock as death comes for me.

Meanwhile, I wait in the condemned cell, looking out at the world through the bars. From this vantage point, I see a world which is drugged to prevent any thought of death. It is as if there is a maniacal killer at large, the fear of whom is so great that people pretend that he does not exist.

Yet only from this cell, from this understanding of my own mortality, can I see the world with its cloak of pretence removed. Today, my cell overlooks the pavement in front of the Praetorium. A crowd is arriving. Never have I seen such a thirst for blood. They have dragged a young man here to

ask Pilate to crucify him. Pilate comes out protected by
guards. 'What charge do you bring?' asks Pilate.

They give no direct answer but say sarcastically, 'If he
weren't a criminal, he wouldn't be here.' Pilate lacks
patience when it comes to sorting out religious squabbles.

'Don't waste my time!' he says. 'Try him yourself!'

'But we can't sentence him to death!'

Pilate takes the young prisoner inside for questioning.
There can be no fair hearing in the presence of the mob.
Then Pilate reappears without the prisoner and says, 'I find
no case against him.'

The crowd is enraged and cries all the louder for blood.

Musa winds along a path across a field of with-
ered sorghum. Even if the rain comes, he cannot wait the
two months until harvest. By then he and Rahila, his six-
year-old daughter, will have died of starvation. On his head
is a bundle tied in a blanket. Rahila is barefoot, wearing
only a mottled blue dress. On her head is a five-litre can of
water. Musa turns and takes a last look at the huts that
have been his home for 15 years. With the help of friends,
he built them and thatched them. His five children were
born there. His wife and four of them are buried there.

He is now taking Rahila over scorched hills and plains to
the safety of the town 80 miles away. He has heard that the
brothers at the mission are giving away food. Walking is an
effort for both himself and Rahila. Two years ago, he could
carry a sack of grain to the village market 15 miles away
and then walk back the same evening. His limbs were
sturdy. Now, they resemble the branch he is using as a staff.
Rahila, too, was once strong and healthy. Now, her cheeks
are hollow and her eyes sunken. A distance of 80 miles is a
long way without food but, perhaps, someone will take pity
on the way.

I am still peering out through the bars watching the mob. Pilate is coming outside again followed by none other than Tiberias Caesar! What is he doing here? He will put an end to this stupidity. Then my eyes focus. It is not laurel on his head but acacia. And the purple toga is oozing with the blood of a scourging. It is not Caesar but the prisoner, his face running with blood. Pilate bellows, 'Here's the man!' The crowd is now beside itself. 'Take him yourselves and crucify him: I find no case against him.'

The crowd replies, 'We have a law, and according to that law he ought to be put to death.' Pilate looks worried and takes the young man inside.

Miles O'Shea puts down his knife and fork. As the waiter collects the plate, Miles says, 'Those pancakes were delicious.' His gratitude belies the fact that he had pancakes for breakfast and pancakes last night when he arrived. He is the only guest in the town's only guest house – a town and a guest house almost out of food.

This morning, Miles went to the military headquarters and then to see the brothers at the mission. He is a field worker with a relief organisation and is here to ascertain the need caused by the drought. He puts on his white cotton cap and makes his way on foot to the northern edge of the town. He follows the pot-holed ribbon of tarmac that is the main street. There are people about but no traffic apart from the odd bicycle and military vehicle. On either side of the street are mud and breeze block stores. There are no shop windows, just doorways with wooden and enamel placards above them advertising 'Pepsi', 'Tate and Lyle', 'Sunlight', and 'Persil'. Few of the stores have provisions left, though one of them has slabs of washing soap on a trestle table outside. Further along, a woman is cooking over an open fire. Miles is tempted to buy from her but changes his mind. A metal tray is resting on the embers with pancakes cooking on it.

He reaches the edge of the town. Tents made of plastic sheeting and cardboard stretch a quarter of a mile towards the sparse savannah. A hot wind blows from the north raising the dust and rattling the plastic of the makeshift homes. The breeze is like the draught from an oven though the smell is not so pleasing. A gust whips up a cloud of grit and sweeps it like a burst of rain across the hovels. It is the wet season but that is the nearest thing they have had to a drenching.

There are neither chickens, goats, dogs nor donkeys, just forlorn people. Men in long white robes sit on their heels under a tree. Women are tending fires in the manner they used to when there was food to cook. Small children are lying on a grass mat shaded by green bin liners tied together and supported by poles. Older children are queuing at the water tank – a six-foot cube of sheet metal with an opening in the top and a tap on the side. The army comes each morning to fill it. Once a day, brothers from the mission bring gruel but their supplies are almost out and the number of people to be fed grows daily.

Miles is soon surrounded by hands held out for food. A man with a wound under his eye asks for medicine. A naked boy of five, with a running nose and skin white with dust, holds out his hands for bread. A woman carrying a sick toddler asks for milk. People press in on every side. All are so thin and sickly that they look near to death. He tries to brush them away but the more steps he takes the more people he gathers. Then, in the distance, thirty people emerge from the bush. They trundle towards the makeshift tents and then weave between them asking where to find water. They look too thin to stand but they are carrying babies, straw mats and bundles. Among them is Rahila, the little girl with the mottled blue dress and sunken eyes. Musa, her father, did not make it.

Miles turns to make his way back to the town but cannot move for the crowd. Then, a burst of automatic gunfire sends the throng shrieking away. Some throw themselves to the ground. Others stumble as they try to run. Miles dives behind a cardboard hovel and then hears raucous male laughter. 'Englishman', shouts a voice, 'come here!' There is an open-backed lorry on the edge of the camp. On it is a handful of soldiers. They had seen Miles' predicament and had fired in the air to disperse the crowd.

At four o'clock in the afternoon, as previously arranged with the military, Miles goes to their local headquarters in the centre of the town to radio a request for aid to his colleague in the capital. The walls of the radio room are bare mud. The only furniture is a desk and chair. On the desk is a transmitter in a dark green metal case. Above it, on the wall, is a poster of Michael Jackson. There are no windows. The only light comes from a desk lamp, leaving most of the room in darkness. A young major is seated, wearing headphones and speaking into the microphone. Moments later, Miles has taken his place and is radioing the request.

He vouches for the ability of the brothers at the mission to administer the aid and reads out a list of food and medical supplies. His colleague says, 'Subject to military clearance, one month's supplies will be on their way within 24 hours and should arrive in two-and-a-half days. Sorry, we can't send more at this stage. The picture we're building is of a catastrophe greater than we have seen. The crisis extends beyond this country. Unless the West makes a swift response, our regional food stocks will be depleted in weeks. And, Miles, drive to Bharga tomorrow as arranged. The Finnish Lutherans are reporting an influx of refugees.'

At the relief organisation's HQ in Britain, an appeal is orchestrated. An adequate response to the crisis would use up the organisation's reserves three times over. A multi-pronged campaign has been devised. A TV crew is flying out. TV coverage will then be backed up with press advertising and a mail-shot to known supporters. The envelopes will have printed on them in red: 'Urgent! Crisis in Africa!'

Pilate is re-emerging alone. I press close to the bars; there is so much noise that it is difficult to hear him. He is telling them that the prisoner must go free. Then they scream, 'Anyone who claims to be king is an enemy of Caesar's. Set the man free and you are Caesar's enemy, too!' Pilate sends a guard inside.

It is June 1991. I have just arrived at the municipal campsite in Tamanrasset, Southern Algeria. Tomorrow, I will drive the 50 miles to Mount Assékrem to the hermitage of Charles de Foucauld. But first, today, I need bread. The camp office is closed, so I walk to a building 50 yards away hoping that it is the site shop. It turns out to be the toilet block. Approaching it is a tall, muscular African in his early thirties carrying a bucket. I ask him where I can buy bread. He says he will take me. On the way he tells me that he is Jimmy Hiksy, from Ghana. He speaks eight languages, including English, French, German, Italian and Arabic, but has ended up as a lavatory cleaner in the middle of nowhere. I buy bread, we exchange addresses and he goes back to his bucket.

The prisoner is brought out and pushed onto a chair. 'Here is your king!' says Pilate.
The crowd is furious.
'Away with him! Crucify him!'
But Pilate replies, 'Shall I crucify your king?'
They answer, 'We have no king but Caesar.'

We have just finished our evening meal at the vicarage. While we are clearing up the kitchen, I switch on the television to catch the headlines to see if the news is going to be worth watching. Job losses, an IRA bomb and famine in Africa. Nothing much, so I switch it off.

A few days later at ten minutes to nine in the morning, I sit at my desk, scanning the day's post to see which I should open first. I start with a letter from Niamey in Niger. It is from Jimmy Hiksy, the lavatory cleaner I met in Tamanrasset. He writes that he has been deported from Algeria, spent three days without food or money at the Niger border and then hitchhiked to Niamey, the capital. He has borrowed a little money, but at the time of writing, it has almost run out. He might already be starving. He asks me for £100. This will repay the loan, buy him food and get him back to his village in Ghana.

I scribble a note to him saying that I have not got £100. This is not strictly true and I have an uneasy conscience. I am not able to tell him that I put my holiday before his basic needs. I take a £10 note out of my wallet and enclose it with the letter.

The rest of the day's mail remains unopened. I scan the envelopes to see which to open next. I am helped by the two envelopes which say on the outside what is on the inside. One of them is from an animal rights organisation; the other is marked 'Urgent! Crisis in Africa!'. I throw them unopened in the bin. My conscience niggles me.

'Lord', I say, 'I'm always giving. I tithe my income and give a little besides.'

'You keep the Old Testament Law, but once you've given your ten per cent, you feel free of any obligation. Live by grace, not by law!'

'If I lived by grace, I'd have nothing left. I'd rather increase my giving by a few percent and then I'd know where I stood.'

'You don't get the point. You are using the Law to protect your standard of living. You use it to safeguard your money, to keep yourself from being my disciple. Remind me to send you some dill and cumin seeds!' I ferret around in my desk drawer and take out a Charities' Aid Foundation cheque book. 'You're not going to send one of those cheques are you? That's money you've already laid aside to be given away!'

'That's all I can afford! I've just sent Jimmy Hiksy £10 and that wasn't part of my tithe!'

It is Saturday 27 February 1993. I am sitting in a bazaar in the old city of Jerusalem. I am browsing outside when the proprietor tries to sell me a jug made of Jerusalem glass. I tell him that I have spent up. I then ask him what it is like living in Jerusalem.

'This is what it is like', he says, beckoning me inside the shop and pointing to a photograph hanging on the wall. It is a picture of a young man smiling and leaning against a motor car. 'We had five daughters and a son called Ismail.' He points to the young man in the photograph. 'He studied in Newcastle, England. He was going to be a chemical engineer. He gained a first-class honours degree. Three weeks after he returned, he was dead. He had gone to see my brother in Nablus. He was shot. They said he was a terrorist.'

My conscience burns. I cannot tell him that I am chairman of the North-West Friends of Israel. I cannot tell him that while holding that post I have never once criticised the Israeli occupation.

Rahila holds out her bowl. Only one ladleful, half rations. If the convoy hasn't arrived by Friday, she will be on quarter rations. If it hasn't arrived in ten days, she will have no food at all.

The mob is on the point of riot. 'What harm has he done?' demands Pilate. I press close to the bars.

'If the prisoner lives, my income will be reduced', screams one.

'My van is ten years old! I need a new one! Crucify!'

'I couldn't live on lentils. If he lives, I couldn't afford meat!'

'I like to go out for a meal! Away with him!'

'It's better that this one dies, so that we can all be better off.' Then, with one voice they cry, 'Away with him! Away with him! Crucify!'

As much as I hate their barbarism, I admit that their logic is faultless. They are more honest than I. I want to keep my vehicle and go on holiday. I have not condemned the prisoner with my mouth. I do not have the integrity of the mob, but I have passed the death sentence with my deeds.

Pilate calls for water to wash his hands. The crowd shouts, 'His blood be upon us', but I am too cowardly to join my voice with theirs. I'd rather ask Pilate for his bowl and towel.

As the prisoner is led away, I recognise him. It is Jimmy Hiksy, the cleaner from Tamanrasset. Then, I notice that there are three crosses lying by the wall. Pilate clears his throat and shouts, 'Bring the remaining prisoners.'

Emerging from the shadows, two prisoners are led by guards. One of them is Ismail, the shopkeeper's son. Shackled to him is a little girl with sunken eyes and a blue mottled robe. The crowd roars for blood but I have no stomach for this scene. I let go of the bars and turn my head. A key turns in the lock and the cell door opens. A voice speaks to me, 'Hey you, Barabbas, you're free.'

> *Lord, the life I have received from you was at the cost of your own. My lifestyle is paid for by the lives of others and by you in them. I am surrounded by luxuries which if given up would save others. If I lived without them I could free others from the sentence of death. I go on sinning knowing what I do. I condemn you daily.*

2   Jesus Takes Up His Cross

'Come to me, all you who labour and are
overburdened, and I will give you rest.
Shoulder my yoke and learn from me, for I
am gentle and humble in heart, and you will
find rest for your souls. Yes, my yoke is easy
and my burden light.'

(Matthew 11:28–30)

Lord Jesus, I will shoulder your yoke and learn
from you. I will follow you anywhere. Wherever you lead, I
will go. Like the twelve, I will be your student. If we face
opposition from Pharisees, you can outwit them. If they try
to throw us over a cliff, we can turn and walk through
them. With you, I can make whole the sick and disturbed.
We can calm stormy seas and walk on water. No challenge
is too great. I am safe with you. I will go anywhere for you,
do anything for you.

I am sitting on the step of the Ecce Homo Convent in that narrow Jerusalem street called the Via Dolorosa. The world is passing by – people from many nations.
Three yards from me across the street is a bazaar selling
Jerusalem glass, carvings out of olive wood and ecclesiasti-
cal stoles which hang brightly outside. It is quarter to three
on the afternoon of Friday 26 February. This is the day I
have been waiting for. At three o'clock, so I'm told, Franciscans begin the Stations of the Cross from this spot. I came
to Israel primarily to be with them today. I am joined by
others who lean against the stone wall of the convent or

browse in one of the bazaars. At five minutes to three there is no sign of the Franciscans. I approach a tall American wearing khaki trousers and a bush hat. It is Bill, the American Roman Catholic priest whom I met yesterday at a refugee camp in the West Bank. 'Is this where the Stations of the Cross begin?' Before he can reply, we see four Franciscans in their brown habits coming up the street. Two of them are carrying crosses. The crosses are almost six foot tall but light enough to be carried in one hand.

The Franciscans pass us, but after a few yards walk from the street up a long stone ramp into a courtyard, with me and a couple of dozen others in pursuit. The courtyard is that of the Omariye College. It is bordered by buildings and high walls, all built of the same beige Jerusalem stone. Over 200 people are already here. There is the loud background noise of the three o'clock call to prayer from the minaret which stands at one corner of the courtyard. The crowd comprises Franciscans, some nuns in black habits, Japanese, Germans, Italians, French, English, Americans and others whose nationality I cannot discern. There is a party atmosphere with people chatting in groups and enjoying the sunshine. An overweight Italian wearing a flat cap goes to one of the Franciscans and borrows a cross to have his photograph taken. He rests the cross over his shoulder while he wears an enormous smile and has a cigarette dangling from his mouth. The photographer cracks a joke and the man carrying the cross laughs heartily. Then a succession of others come to take up the cross. I can't believe it. Each one of them is smiling as he poses as the man of sorrows.

The crosses are handed back to the Franciscans. They stand facing the courtyard wall and the devotions begin. Prayer and scripture is offered in Latin, Arabic and English. I can see no plaque or picture marking the Station. They seem to be talking to the wall. We move from the first Station, down the stone ramp back onto the Via Dolorosa to the second Station outside the Ecce Homo Convent.

Those leading the prayers face the wall. I can hear, but only just. The street was busy before the pilgrims flooded onto it. Now it is clogged with 200 or 300 people, each trying to press nearer to the scene of devotion.

The procession moves off to the third Station, where above the door of the Polish chapel is a sculpture of Jesus falling under the weight of the cross. I can't see it but I know it's there. I'm looking at a photograph in a leaflet I've bought. I can't hear a word. I'm stuck 30 yards from the Station, pinned by the crowd against the wall.

Then the crowd, so dense as to appear impenetrable, becomes agitated. It is being pushed back against its desired direction of flow. The El Aqsa Mosque has let out and hundreds of Muslims flood the street, flushing before them the Christian pilgrims. I'm pushed back another 30 yards before taking refuge in a doorway. For five minutes I can't move as the stream pushes past. It is the first Friday of Ramadan, so there are more worshippers than usual. By the time that we get moving again, we have lost the Franciscans. I turn to people and ask, 'Which way?' The pilgrims near me look as puzzled as I feel. A Palestinian points round a corner and says, 'This way.'

We try to rush, but the street is still thick with people. Off we press, past bazaars and coffee shops, hoping to catch a glimpse of the tail end of the procession. Then I see some nuns and follow them. With effort, rudely squeezing past people, I catch them up, only to find that they are not nuns but Palestinian women whose dress is similar.

At last, I can see the Franciscans 50 yards ahead at the eighth Station but I am not near enough to hear. I'm getting closer when a second mosque empties pushing me back again. This time I shelter from the flood by stepping into a bazaar. 'Please, sir', says the proprietor, 'may I show you this beautiful carpet. Only 2,000 shekels.' The carpet is rolled up on the floor near shelves bearing glass and copper.

'No thank you', I say. 'I'm doing the Stations of the Cross. I'm just waiting until the crowd has passed.'

'Then, sir, look at this.' He picks up a nativity scene in olive wood. 'This was carved by my own father in Bethlehem.'

'I must be going', I say, but the crowd is such that I cannot get back onto the street.

'Please, sir, give me 150 shekels for this beautiful nativity.' Then his voice becomes harsh. 'Jerusalem is crowded, but nobody is going in the shops. Nobody buys. My business is being ruined. Tourists are told not to shop here because we are supposed to be terrorists. I am just a simple man with a family to keep.' All the time my back is to him while I wait for a gap in the crowd. 'Please, sir, have you a wife? I have beautiful jewellery.'

I am still trying to get back on the street and he is still talking to me. 'They are ruining our trade. They say it is unsafe for tourists in the old city. There is a heavy tax for living here. It is that you are deprived of your liberty. They are driving us out of our country. We were born here. This is our land but they will not be happy until the last one of us is gone.'

There is then a gap in the crowd. I squeeze into it and push on. I hear someone say, 'Which way did they go?' Pilgrims identify each other and then give chase. I arrive at the Basilica of the Holy Sepulchre shoulder to shoulder with Bill, the Roman Catholic priest. We are now almost running as we approach the building. 'The last five Stations are inside', he says. But before we get to the door, two Franciscans walk out of it, one of them lighting a cigarette.

'Is it finished?' I ask them. They nod and walk off. Behind them are two tourists with cameras, one of them bringing one of the crosses out of the Basilica. They take turns to be photographed with it. Each of them smiles as he poses as the man of sorrows.

Lord Jesus, I will follow you anywhere, do anything for you. Your burden is easy and your yoke is light.

The master is weak through loss of blood. He has been up all night, scourged, and beaten. The soldiers lead him to a heavy wooden cross lying on the ground. He is told to pick it up. This act, like that of forcing men to dig their own graves, is designed to humiliate. He has already borne their taunts when they dressed him in purple. At the end of this long walk, he will bear them again when they strip him of his clothes. But though they try, they cannot prevent him from going to his death with dignity.

He stoops, puts his hands under the timber and lifts but he is struggling. He is too weak to lift it higher than his waist. The crowd laughs as if it were comedy. It is great entertainment. A soldier whips him to encourage him to get it on his shoulder, but it is no good. Someone will have to help. They manhandle it into position. With the crowd in carnival mood, the procession sets off.

The prisoner is surrounded by people, but never has anyone been so alone. Only he knows the full horror. We look on, pitying, but I say, 'Thank God it's not me.' I feel like a child who has stolen from the pantry only to find that his brother has been blamed and punished. The guilt is uncomfortable but I am relieved. It is my cross that he carries. It is my shame that he suffers.

Lord Jesus, I will follow you anywhere, do anything for you. Your burden is easy and your yoke is light.

'Geoff, you choose the scriptures selectively. If I choose to place a light burden upon you that is up to me. But from your point of view, hear this: If anyone would come after me, then he must be willing to take up his cross. As a disciple, you can aspire to great things, but one thing I ask: Pick up your cross and follow me.

'There are millions of people prepared to follow me, that is until it is time to pick up the cross. Then they disappear.

You thought that the Stations of the Cross with the Franciscans was a farce. The crosses were light. Some of those who carried them wore beaming smiles. Don't you understand that those Stations are true to life? Is the cross that you carry for me any heavier than those taken down the Via Dolorosa every Friday? Is your smile any less broad than theirs?'

Lord, give me the courage I need to be your disciple.

3 Jesus Falls for the First Time

> *The woman saw that the tree was good to eat*
> *and pleasing to the eye, and that it was*
> *enticing for the wisdom that it could give. So*
> *she took some of its fruit and ate it. She also*
> *gave some to her husband who was with her,*
> *and he ate it.*
>
> (Genesis 3:6)

When I sin, Jesus falls under the weight of it, for I carry not my own sin. The burden is not only too great for me to bear, it is too great even for him. The first time I became aware of this, I vowed never to sin again. The vow, like a New Year's resolution, was not long kept and I fell again. When I, like Adam, fell, Jesus fell.

I am mystified by this twist of cause and effect. I cannot see the connection. There is no logic, but one thing I know: I am the cause and he bears the effect. Ezekiel says that it is no longer true that fathers eat sour grapes to see their children's teeth set on edge. Why is it then that my Lord tastes the bitterness of the cup I drink?

If only I could carry the weight of my own misdeeds. If I were allowed to try, I would be crushed out of existence. His love is such that he takes my burden, a burden too great for even him. I sin and he falls.

> *When I first gave you my burdens, I thought*
> *that you would toss them into the lake of fire*
> *to be consumed or that you would bury them*
> *in the deepest sea. To see you bowed down*

*under their weight, suffering, bleeding, and
crushed makes me unable to look at you.
What have I done? I wish I could say that I
will ease your load by never placing another
one on you, but I know that before long I will
fall and drag you to the floor with me. Lord,
have mercy.*

4   Jesus Meets His Mother

*On the third day, there was a wedding at Cana
in Galilee. The mother of Jesus was there,
and Jesus and his disciples had also been
invited. And they ran out of wine, since the
wine provided for the feast had all been used,
and the mother of Jesus said to him, 'They
have no wine.' Jesus said, 'Woman, what do
you want from me? My hour has not come
yet.'*

(John 2:1–4)

A Sunday morning in January 1993 after the
service, I am in the church hall drinking a cup of tea,
chatting to members of the congregation. One of them says,
'Your mother was on Piccadilly Radio last night.' I look
puzzled. 'It was a phone-in programme. She was talking
about you and all your wonderful achievements.' The tea
which I am drinking is almost sprayed across the room. The
embarrassment is too much. Not much is harder to bear
than the adulation of a proud parent. I am quite capable of
boasting, but one thing that makes me cringe more than
anything else is my mother blowing my trumpet for me.

It is 1993 and my father is ill in hospital. In introducing
me to a nurse, my mother tells her with great pride that I
am an area dean and that I have just returned from walking
up Sca Fell Pike. She makes it sound as if I have climbed
Everest in my bare feet. I escape by going to the coffee
machine down the corridor.

The same month, I receive a letter from the incumbent of
a church in a Cheshire town, 30 miles away. I neither know

him, his church nor his town, but he is inviting me to preach. My mother has a friend in his congregation. My mother has worked out a plan so that her friend can hear me preach. She asks her friend to get the vicar to invite me.

I feel like a five-year-old whose mother is telling her friends how well he's doing at school. I want to say, 'Mother, I've grown up. Please don't make me feel uncomfortable.' But, awkward as I feel, I comply. She is my mother after all.

Jesus is enjoying the wedding when the wine runs out. His mother is proud of him. His birth was miraculous, announced by an archangel and heralded by a star. He was visited by eastern sages. Old Simeon and latterly John the Baptist recognised him for who he was. If any mother has cause to be proud, it is she. Like any mother, she has ambitions for her son.

His ministry has already begun. He has recruited disciples. He is poised to usher in the Kingdom with signs and wonders. It is nearly the moment, but not quite. 'Woman, what has it got to do with you? It's not time for my glory to be seen.' His mother is proudly waiting for signs of the Kingdom. She cannot wait. She prompts him by means of the steward. Then, like someone lighting touch paper, she stands back. It is a proud moment.

Mary, you are seeking your son's glory. Don't you understand that when his glory is truly seen, you will be cut to the heart?

The Palestinian shopkeeper has tears in his eyes as he looks at the photograph of Ismail, his son. He turns to me. 'Would you like coffee?' he asks. I accept and am offered a stool. The man goes through a door at the back. All around me are shelves laden with trinkets and jewellery. I am then startled. I hadn't noticed a woman sitting at the bottom end of the shop. I assume that it is his wife. I try to speak to the woman, but she speaks no English. Ten minutes later the husband returns with a metal tray. 'Please', he says, offering me the tiny mug of what looks like hot brown mud.

'No sugar, thank you', I say.

'When Ismail was a child, he was quick and bright. He was kind and helpful. One day he could have changed the world. He was intelligent, too. There was no work for him, so we planned for him to help in the shop while he was looking for a job. My brother lives in Nablus. He is poor. Sometimes I used to take food for his family and clothes for his children. Then, when Ismail came back from England, I asked him to take a few things for him. He set off in my car, but we never saw him again. He was shot.'

'Was he a terrorist?'

'Everyone here will do anything to fight for our freedom. We were born in this land. Why should these people who have come from Europe tell us what to do? Why should they make us pay tax? Why should we need permits from them? The Israeli settlers can carry arms. When they shoot us it's difficult to get justice. They said that my son was carrying arms.' Tears come to the old man's eyes. 'I told him only to be involved in peaceful protest. I told him that it is better to face a lion than to fight the Israelis. We had arranged for him to be married. We were looking forward to having grandchildren. He chose his way and we could not stop him.'

As he talks, my heart cries out to God for an end to pain and conflict in this land. Today's *Jerusalem Post* tells me there has been some progress in the Israeli/Palestinian peace talks. If, by a miracle, they reach agreement, it will not bring back Ismail, nor assuage the old man's grief.

Bernard had been ordained for 12 years. One day, he turned up on his mother's doorstep. 'May I have my room back?' he asked. 'I've left the ministry.'

He did not explain why. No one had been more proud than his mother. She had watched his vocation proved and tested by the Church. He had gone through theological college with flying colours. He was a popular curate and an even more popular parish priest. The parishioners idolised him. His mother thought that one day he might become an archdeacon or bishop. There were photographs of him everywhere in her house.

Bernard's resignation was too hard for her to face. He was living with her permanently, but she told everyone that he had not been well and that he was convalescing. 'It won't be long before the bishop offers him another church.' He was constantly drunk, but she refused to notice, waiting on him hand and foot. She was sure that the cause of the 'breakdown' was overwork. The laity in his parish had been difficult to handle. Had he challenged them one time too many? She was angry at those who had done this to her son. 'Take a long rest', she said, 'and then go back.' When he told her that he was finished with the Church, she was inconsolable. She had invested her hope and her pride in him. Bernard later said that her grief was worse than if he had died. Night after night he heard her weeping.

Mary meets her son on the Via Dolorosa. Can we pretend that she understands what this passion is all about? Can we pretend that she accepts that good will come of it? For her, this is blacker than any tragedy. This is failure greater than any failure. Her husband is dead and now her son is taking his last steps. How can he do this to her? How could he have challenged the world knowing that it would come to this?

Mary sums up the anguish of parents who see their hopes for their children dashed. 'I wanted my son to be a doctor', says one, 'but he preferred discos to studying. He's had four jobs in a year and now he works in a warehouse.'

'My daughter won the maths prize in the fourth year. She

wanted to work in a bank – that was until she met her boyfriend. Now she smokes, drinks and works in a supermarket.'

Mary sees her son walking to his death. 'I had such hopes for you. What have you done? You have gone too far. You have challenged the wrong people.'

'Woman, what has it got to do with you? When I was young, you dressed me and put on my belt. You told me where I should go and where I should not go. Now I am a man, I can make up my own mind. This is the way I have chosen.'

Lord, no one meeting Jesus on the way to the cross could have seen anything other than tragedy. To have suggested at that point that his suffering was his glory or that it might become a triumph was ludicrous. And yet what seemed ludicrous was not so. His suffering was victory greater than any other.

Who are we to judge our children's failures and successes? How do we know what good may come? Give us a love for our children without ambition.

5 Simon Carries the Cross of Jesus

As they were leading him away they seized on a man, Simon from Cyrene, who was coming in from the country, and made him shoulder the cross and carry it behind Jesus.

(Luke 23:26)

It is a Tuesday afternoon, 1971. I am wearing a suit and a dog collar, door-to-door visiting in the back streets of the parish where I am curate. I tell each householder that I am from the church and that I have called to introduce myself. I am told that it is nice to meet me and then I hear, 'Come back when the wife's in.' Or, 'I'm a Catholic.' Or, 'I'm getting ready to go out.' Or, 'I'm in the middle of getting my husband's tea ready.'

'A few more doors', I think, 'and I'll go and see if my wife has my meal ready.' I do not want to be late. We're having lamb cutlets for tea, a treat provided by my mother-in-law. A door opens and an eighteen-year-old Indian boy stands beaming at me. I introduce myself. 'Come in Mr Geoff', he says.

'Not Mr Geoff, just Geoff.'

'OK, Mr Geoff.' I follow him down the narrow hallway into the first room on the left. 'This is my room', he says proudly. 'Isn't it wonderful?' It hasn't been decorated for years. There is no carpet, only cracked linoleum which looks as if it has been there since the 1920s. We both sit on the bed – there are no chairs. Neither are there pictures on the wall, other than a poster of Elvis Presley. The only item of furniture is a card table on top of which is a record player. Beside it on the floor is a pile of records. Nazir has a brightness which more than compensates for the drabness of the room. He explains that his family has been in England only a month.

'Forgive me a moment', he says. Springing to his feet, he goes to the door, puts his head into the hall and shouts something in a language which I later learn is Kachi. He sits back beside me. 'I've just asked mother to make some tea.'

'It must be quick', I say. 'I am going soon for my meal.'

'But you have only just arrived. Tell me, Mr Geoff, do you like Elvis Presley?'

'It depends what he's singing', I say, trying to hide my loathing of the King of Rock. Nazir pulls a portable tape recorder from under the bed and switches it on. 'This is me and Elvis singing together.' He has recorded himself singing with an LP of Elvis's greatest hits. Then he sings in the manner of Indian music, bending the notes. 'Since my baby left, I've found a new place to dwell. It's down at the end of Lonely Street at Heartbreak Hotel. I feel so lonely.'

After half an hour, I apologise and say that I am now late and that I must be going. 'Oh, please, Mr Geoff. My mother is making tea.' Fifteen minutes later, I have learned all about him, his parents, brothers and sister, but still the tea has not arrived. The lamb cutlets will be drying up waiting for me in the oven. I stand to leave just as his mother brings in a tray bearing two mugs of tea and eight pieces of buttered toast on a plate. I sit back on the bed to drink it and apologise that I can only eat one piece of toast as my meal will be ready at home. The tea has been made half with milk, half with water, and a mug of sugar, all of which has been boiled with loose tea in a saucepan for half an hour.

Nazir is talking while I eat the toast. 'Aren't you going to have a piece?' I ask.

'No, thank you. I have taken food already.' Over the next 20 minutes, I am coaxed into eating four more slices. Oh dear, I will be in trouble at home.

During the next few months I get to know Nazir and his family well and I grow to like the strange tea. Together we open an Asian youth club in the church hall. The club is so well respected that parents allow their daughters to come. Then the Muslim Indian community invites me to visit one of their sick and to pray for her. There are invitations to attend celebrations and weddings, but as closely as I am involved with them, we rarely talk about religion. They are Muslim and I want to share my faith in Jesus with them, but I know that if I do I might ruin everything. I am hoping either that my life might be testimony enough or else I will be given the opportunity to speak.

When I move out of the neighbourhood in 1974, my contact with the Asian community is not much diminished. I am still invited to their homes. Employers write and ask me to give them references. Now and then, Special Branch asks me to vouch for those who are applying for naturalisation. And Nazir continues to come to my home to practise on my piano and to teach me Urdu.

The soldiers are impatient. Jesus has stopped to talk to his mother. They push him to get him moving, but he almost falls. She walks with him, knowing that if he stumbles she will be unable to prevent the timber from crashing on top of him.

In October 1986, I and 50 other clergy are invited by the Israelis to a meal and tourist promotion at the Grand Hotel, Manchester. My wife is unable to come with me, so I take Ron, a member of my congregation. He is married with three children and earns only a third of the national average wage. He can't afford much entertainment so the evening will be a treat.

The meal is even more sumptuous than I had anticipated. After it, we are seated in rows and told what a wonderful place Israel is, and how, for as little as £500, we can go on a pilgrimage there. Ron, sitting next to me, can't afford £100, let alone £500. For that matter nor could most of my congregation. Many are on the dole or receiving a pension. Some are single parents; others are chronically sick. If only I could get them there cheaply. While the salesman is still talking, I work it out. I'll borrow a bus and camping gear, go overland to South-East Europe and catch a ferry. I reckon I can do it. It will be a 31 day tour for £200 a head. For those who can't afford it we'll raise cash to subsidise them.

When I tell the congregation of my plans, their reaction ranges from enthusiasm to, 'You're nuts', or 'This can't be the will of God', but there is no problem in finding recruits. There are fifty people who sign up to go, many of whom have not only never been abroad before, but have rarely been on any sort of holiday.

Preparation is a nightmare. Finding an available bus, let alone doing the paperwork to take it through 11 different countries, is an ordeal I vow never to repeat. We beg and borrow food and equipment, but towards the end, we are still short of some essentials, one of which is cash. If we don't find it, I will be blamed for raising and dashing the hopes of 50 people.

There is much prayer, but I have to agree with the members of my congregation who say that the venture is fool-hardy and has the potential for causing immense pain. Unless we find all that we need, we will not be going. We have been preparing for two years and are only two months away from the date of departure, but still we are unable to say for definite that we are going. The few employed people who are going hound me daily. They have gone to great lengths to get time off work for a pilgrimage which may never take place.

One year, in One World Week, I organise an overseas evening in my church hall. Christians from many nations will be there. Two days before the event, the folk group that we have booked backs out. I spend an hour trying to find a replacement. When I have run out of ideas, the phone rings. It is Nazir, the Indian who sings like Elvis. He is arranging to come to my house to practise on the piano. 'Nazir', I ask, 'you couldn't bring a few of your friends to church on Thursday and perform for us, could you?' He is delighted and accepts.

Jesus is near to collapse. The soldiers look concerned, not that they are concerned for him. They want to get to Golgotha quickly to get the job done.

We still need money to take the bus to Israel. The departure date is drawing near. I am still being harassed by those who want to know for certain if we are going. Then, one morning a letter lands on my mat. In it there is a cheque from a Jewish businessman, Sir Sidney Hamburger. It is enough to make the trip viable.

Jesus stumbles again and almost falls. Mary's eyes meet those of one of the soldiers. He summons a man from Cyrene. The soldiers take the weight of the cross while Simon takes the place of Jesus. The macabre procession continues on its way.

The man from Cyrene is a foreigner and a pagan. Jesus has many disciples who love him. Yet it is this pagan and foreigner that is called upon to help. And so when the Christian community is too weak to provide musicians for a Christian event, a Muslim volunteers. When the Body of Christ is too poor to carry its own poor, it is a Jew who furthers the Christian cause.

After Simon carried the cross, he was never the same again. He and his sons came to faith in Christ. Can I dare hope that Nazir and Sir Sidney Hamburger will come to faith in the same way?

Lord, I don't know what to tell Nazir. If I tell him about you, if I tell him that you are the truth then I imply that his beliefs are founded on untruth. If I tell him that you are the one true light, then I imply that Mohammed is an impostor. If I tell him that you are the way then I am saying that his way of life, his culture, his family traditions lead nowhere.

I know and love his family. They are such warm people. Their traditions bind people together in a way that Christianity in our culture ought to, but does not. If I preached your gospel it would bring division and pain.

If he came to know you, he would not be able to get down and pray with his father and brothers. He would neither keep Ramadan nor celebrate the feast of Id. His parents, brothers and sisters, grandmother, nephews and nieces would ask, 'Why has Nazir rejected us? Does he think that he is better than we are? Does he think that English culture is superior to ours?' Lord, Islam and his way of life are so bound together that he would not be able to separate them.

I am torn. I know that I am denying him access to you, the Lord of the universe. I know that you are the author of all that is good in his way of life and religion. Yet, if he comes to know you as you are in Christ, all those good things will be replaced by pain and division.

Lord, it might be a price that he is willing to pay, but I'm not prepared to give him the option just yet. I don't want to be responsible for hurting people I love.

Sir Sidney Hamburger's enthusiasm for the pilgrimage matches my own and we become friends. Through him, I meet the Israeli Ambassadors, famous politicians and scientists. Jesus is his Messiah, but as much as I want to tell him, I do not want to offend. And, I guess, he already knows that I believe that Jesus is the Messiah. So, I wait, strengthening the bonds of friendship, hoping that the opportunity will come. I don't want to browbeat him. But then, one day, I overhear another Christian talking to him. This man is telling him that Christianity is for Christians, Islam is for Muslims and that Judaism is for Jews. I wonder if Sir Sidney thinks that those are my beliefs, too. If he does, then I must open my mouth.

Simon Bashir, a Pakistani Christian, comes to my house as a member of a student mission. He tells me that he used to be a Muslim and now longs to share his faith with other Muslims. He fled Pakistan in fear of his life. He asks me if I can introduce him to any Muslims. A quick phone call and Nazir comes round. Nazir and Simon sit on my settee, discussing religion. After four hours, they shake hands warmly and go home.

It is a triumph. Simon is able to witness to Nazir and we all remain friends. I have been too cautious. Perhaps I could have been more open with Nazir from the start. I now have the courage to speak openly about my faith to Sir Sidney Hamburger, and to Nazir. It is only a matter of time. I am now determined to choose the moment for verbal witness.

December 1988, 'I'm writing Christmas cards. As I push one in an envelope for Nazir, I think, 'Strange! I haven't seen him for ages.' I take the card out of the envelope and scribble a message asking if everything is all right. A year later I still haven't heard from him. I scribble another note. Two months later I meet Simon Bashir.

'Have you seen Nazir recently?' he asks.

'Not for a couple of years', I say.

Simon looks embarrassed. 'I think it's my fault. I sent a

parcel of evangelistic literature to him. It was written in Urdu and was critical of the Koran. His father found it and telephoned me. He said that Nazir was severing relations with me. I am sure that he has cut you off too.'

A letter lands on my mat. It is an invitation from the Hamburgers to go to a function at their home. I accept. Part way through the evening when I'm over-indulging on delicious pastries and Israeli wine, I am thinking about Simon Bashir and Nazir. Dare I risk speaking about my faith in Jesus as Messiah to my Jewish friend? I have already blown it with Nazir. Then I think of the imperative of scripture, 'Woe is me if I preach not the Gospel', and, 'I am not ashamed of the Gospel of Christ'. I am torn.

Then, as if he can read my thoughts, Sir Sidney walks over and says, 'You know Geoff, you're not like most other Christians. You never try to convert me.'

> *Lord, there are other Simons of Cyrene, willing to carry your cross for you. When Christians were unable to help, Nazir stepped in and gave a concert for my church. And when my church's resources were inadequate, it was an Orthodox Jew who stepped in. You chose and called these men as you called Simon of Cyrene.*
>
> *In our evangelism, let us not try to force your hand, but be dependent on your Spirit, knowing that he who calls an unbeliever to carry your cross can bring that unbeliever to faith.*

6   Veronica Wipes the Face of Jesus

He is the image of the unseen God.
(Colossians 1:15)

Bernard takes off his clerical shirt, throws it on the bed and puts on an ordinary shirt and tie. He looks at the untidiness of the bedroom and the clothes strewn around the floor. He walks up to the wardrobe mirror. He has not shaved or washed for two days. He goes downstairs, lights a cigarette, puts on a record of Palestrina's *Gloria* and pours himself almost a fifth of a bottle of vodka which he tops up with tonic.

For the past year, he has been having an affair with a man in his congregation. Racked with guilt, he has now broken off the relationship. He is angry with himself, the Church, God and the world. He tries to reason away his guilt but still it remains. He blames the Church for having imbued him with values in which he no longer believes in his head, but which are an inescapable part of his heart. He is angry with God. St Paul tells him that it is better to marry than burn. 'But what's your advice to me?' asks Bernard bitterly. 'I want to marry a man!'

Having broken off the affair, it is too late to get his life together. For months, he's been drowning his guilt in alcohol. He is in debt and has 'borrowed' almost £2,000 of church money. Bernard has been keeping the church books for the past three months while the treasurer has been ill. The treasurer is now well enough to resume his duties. Bernard is broken and can do nothing other than run.

He puts on his mac, downs the vodka, and goes into his study, takes a long hard look at the bookshelves and the clutter that have been a part of his life for years. He turns to go, but walks back and takes from the desk the copy of the *Book of Common Prayer* that his mother bought him at his ordination. It is leather bound and printed on India paper. For its size, the print is large. He leaves the vicarage and gets into his car with a small suitcase, the prayer book and the remains of the bottle of vodka.

Bernard is loved in his parish. People there say he is the best priest they have ever had. He has only a vague idea of where he will spend the night. He is going out into the wilderness. He has no job and no money. Perhaps out there he will be able to love as he wishes without conscience. Perhaps not. Perhaps he will go back to his mother.

Drunk, he drives to his churchwarden's house and drops two sets of vicarage keys through the letter box, without any note of explanation. Then he begins the two-hour drive to my home to tell me that he is leaving the ministry. Now and then, as he drives, he takes the bottle of vodka from the passenger seat and drinks some. When he arrives at my home, I'm not there but in church officiating at a mid-week service.

He walks in, sweating profusely, and takes a pew next to Sophia, a lady of 76. His eyes are closed and he is trembling. Sophia whispers, asking him if he is all right. He makes no reply. At the end of the service she touches him and he falls sideways along the pew. His face is glistening with sweat.

She dashes to the kitchen while I sit next to him. 'Are you all right, Bernard?' He makes no reply. As yet, I have no idea what the problem is. Sophia appears with a wet tea towel and places it on his head. He opens his eyes and sits up, holding the towel to his brow.

'Let's go to my house', I say to Bernard. The rest of the congregation, Bernard and I walk down the aisle to the north-west door. Phyllis wants a word with me. We chat for a moment, leaving Sophia talking to Bernard.

Although Simon is carrying the cross, Jesus has barely enough strength to walk. He looks as if he has been mauled by a lion. Blood is soaking through his clothes. He wipes his face with his hands, smearing the blood and sweat but not removing it. Blood from his scalp is running down his face and into his eyes. He blinks trying to see. The soldiers manhandle him through the mob. Never has such hatred been unleashed on a man of gentleness and peace. Those who have sympathy for him are either silent or absent.

Three years later, Sophia is housebound. One Tuesday afternoon, I am giving her communion at home. I have just introduced service cards instead of books for house communions. 'I'd rather not use the card, vicar', she says. 'I prefer my prayer book. I like the large print.'

'Was it bought you on a special occasion?'

'No. Do you remember that drunk who came into church about three years ago? He collapsed on the pew, and I put a wet towel on his head to bring him round. During the service, he'd seen me struggling to read the small print. On his way out, he said, "Excuse me. I think you could make use of this", and handed me his prayer book. He said, "It's not stolen. It used to belong to a clergyman." There's something written inside, but I can't quite make it out.'

'May I see it?' I ask. She hands it to me. On the flyleaf it reads, 'Never has a mother been so proud. To Bernard on the occasion of your ordination as deacon.' Then the date is added.

'You know, vicar, it didn't matter that he was a tramp. I always remember those words, "In as much as you do it unto the least of these, you do it unto me". And, do you know, vicar, it sounds silly, but I saw Jesus in his face. It was Jesus giving me that prayer book. He was sort of saying, "You have done me a kindness. I'm going to do something for you." He left me with a reminder.'

Lord, when we help others, we ask no reward other than to see your face.

7   Jesus Falls for the Second Time

He was being wounded for our rebellions,
crushed because of our guilt; the punishment
reconciling us fell on him, and we have been
healed by his bruises.

(Isaiah 53:5)

It is a spring morning in 1891. Three-year-old George with his brothers and sisters are watching their father's coffin being lowered into a grave. After the blessing, the children, now orphans, part tearfully. Three of them are taken by the staff of Dr Barnardo's. Sarah goes to live with Aunt Selina. George goes with Aunt Emily, who has children of her own and only two bedrooms.

Little is known of George's life until he is fifteen when, claiming to be sixteen, he joins the Warwickshire regiment as a bugle boy. Four years later, in 1907, he is posted to India. He is well respected for his good humour, toughness and honesty. Before long, he is boxing for his regiment.

In 1914, the regiment returns home and is sent to the front line. He is wounded, but after convalescence returns to the front. He is wounded again. This time the medics offer to have him posted somewhere in England, but he refuses and asks to go back to his unit. He suffers gassing and is wounded a third time at the battle of the Somme. He is never well enough to return to active service. When he is 32, he marries and leaves the army, but keeps on boxing until he is 45. My father is his first child.

Until I was married, I lived with my parents in a terraced house in Manchester. My grandparents lived across the street and I often popped in to see them. My earliest memory of my grandfather was when I was three. There was little traffic in our street and toddlers played on the pavement. Grandfather worked in the railway goods depot. On summer evenings, when I saw him at the top of the street I ran to him. He picked me up and put me on his shoulders. He was strong and gentle. I trusted him totally. Naughty boys from the next street who tried to bully me were no threat when he was around. On dark nights, we sat by the fire spellbound by his magic. He did conjuring tricks, producing coins, handkerchiefs and eggs out of thin air.

To all the family, he was a hero and a legend in his own time. Everyone looked up to this strong and good man. There was a security in his presence and wisdom in his advice.

It is the end of a hard day. He is in the stern asleep with his head on a cushion. When the storm breaks, the crewmen fear for their lives, as the craft is thrashed by wind and wave. They wake him, accusing him of not caring. With a word from him, the storm abates. With this and many other deeds, he proves himself invincible. They know that so long as they are with him, they are safe.

One day in 1953, when I was eight years old, I came home from school to find that this man whom I had thought invincible was in hospital with pneumonia. We were told that there was no hope for him. He wasn't dead, but we were in mourning. There was denial and disbelief. 'He can't die', we thought. 'He is too much a part of our lives.' As it was, he recovered. 'We were right', we said, 'and the doctors were wrong. They don't understand how strong he is.'

The Via Dolorosa is packed. Children are hawking bread and cooked meat to the onlookers. The soldiers make a way through the people, past the crowded bazaars and eating houses. The condemned man puts one foot in front of the other. He has lost much blood. The wood is cutting into the torn flesh of his shoulders. A few minutes ago he fell. Some people laughed, but those of his followers who had not fled were urging him to get to his feet. Everything he ever taught, everything he ever stood for was at stake. They were desperate for him to get up to prove that he had not lost his power. When he rose to his feet, they murmured, 'We knew he would. Nothing is too difficult for him. He will win through.'

In February 1954, freezing smog blankets Manchester. Grandfather again falls ill. We are allowed to visit the hospital at any time. He is not expected to live. 'He will pull through', we say. We hide our fear with bravado. When he does pull through, we say, 'We knew he'd get better.' What we really mean is that we cannot face the thought of life without him.

The soldiers cut a way through the people. The prisoner is collapsing, but we refuse to admit it. We do not know why he is letting them do this to him. Soon he will use his power and cast off this weight, but then he falls again with the timber crashing on top of him, pinning him to the ground. As he struggles to his feet, we say, 'We knew he would. Nothing is too difficult for him. He will win through.'

Lord Jesus, in the glorious trinity, you are the creator and sustainer of all things. Everything is in subjection to you. Your name is higher than any other.

I understand your strength, but your weakness confuses me. I need you to be strong. The idea of a powerless God terrifies me. I have no strength but yours. I enjoy being strong and confident. I love being in control, rather than being controlled. If you are weak and vulnerable then so must I be. When I saw you fall a second time, I thought I was dreaming. When you got to your feet, I felt immeasurable relief. The God in whom I trust is strong again!

8 Jesus Consoles the Women of Jerusalem

Large numbers of people followed him, and women too who mourned and lamented for him. But Jesus turned to them and said, 'Daughters of Jerusalem, do not weep for me; weep rather for yourselves and for your children.'

(Luke 23:27–8)

It is five o'clock in the afternoon, Wednesday 23 February 1993. I am driving in a rented car into East Jerusalem on my way from Tel Aviv. The traffic is fast-moving and tightly bunched, I keep snatching for the gear stick on the wrong side and am trying to read a map to find the guest house at St George's Cathedral. I mistakenly think that St George's Church in the old city is St George's Cathedral. I've been driving round for an hour trying to reach the wrong building. Eventually, I find myself approaching the Mount of Olives. I drive past a group of children. They give chase and hurl rocks at the car. One of the rocks bounces off the back of the vehicle. I accelerate and arrive at the top of the Mount of Olives from which the old city can be seen across the Kidron Valley. 'There it is, but how do I get there?'

Two Palestinian men are selling postcards just a few yards away. I get out of the car and ask them the way. 'You must be crazy coming here in a rented car from Israel', they say. I look puzzled. 'You have the wrong colour plates. No one comes here with yellow plates. This is occupied territory. You need a car with green plates. The Israeli military have used cars like this for under-cover work. You're lucky our kids haven't turned your car over and set fire to it.' I look horrified. 'If you want to get to the old city, leave your car with us. It will be safe.'

'How much?' I ask.

'Nothing', they say. 'You are our guest.' One of the men sticks out his hand. 'I'm Mike', he says, 'and this is my brother Bassam.' I feel uneasy leaving the car with them, but by the end of the week I have asked them to look after it many times. Rocks have been hurled at the car again and again, but have only made contact once. When driving round East Jerusalem I am a danger to myself and to others, avoiding stones being thrown by driving so fast that no one can see the plates let alone know what colour they are.

I am carrying my briefcase, walking down Radak Street in a quiet neighbourhood of West Jerusalem. The two-storey and three-storey houses are 50 years old with large trees in the gardens. Though it is February, I am warm enough without a jacket. The few passers-by are relaxed. The West Bank seems as far from here as it might do from the suburbs of Nice, Milan and Barcelona, but the residents here could jump in their cars and be there in 15 minutes. They are allowed to travel over the 'green line', but most choose not to. Many of them know more about European cities than they do about Bethlehem. For some of them 'Palestinian' means 'terrorist'.

I have been trying to spot door numbers without success, but then I see the one I've been looking for. There is no plaque on the wall, just a number seven. It is the head-quarters of the World Zionist Organisation. It is 11 a.m. and I have an appointment with Sarah Fleiderman, the deputy director.

I am welcomed into the building by a female secretary and taken down a narrow corridor with boxes of stationery stacked to one side. Sarah's office is five yards along on the right. She is a warm and charming woman in her fifties, an émigrée from Argentina.

I want to talk to her about the plight of Palestinians, but I keep off the subject. I feel powerless. I have not yet met many Palestinians. If I challenge Israel's treatment of them, I will be told that I don't understand. I know the Zionist line. Israel is surrounded by hostile nations, all of whom are allies of the Palestinians. To give the Palestinian people complete freedom would be to invite terrorism on a massive scale. 'We have a right to protect ourselves', Israelis tell me. 'You don't understand what it is like being a nation under siege. Imagine if Wales were the sworn enemy of the rest of Britain. Imagine too if its allies were the rest of Europe. You would deprive the Welsh of certain freedoms. It would be unfair on some law-abiding Welsh people, but we are at war. You interned Germans during the war. We have a right to do the same with Palestinians. We want peace. We are only protecting ourselves.'

But instead, Sarah Fleiderman tells me with enthusiasm of Israel's achievements in irrigation, tree planting and horticulture. 'We lead the world in the genetic engineering of plants. No one can match our crop yields. We have developed trees that produce fruit all year round. And we are not keeping these advances to ourselves. We have scientists who are helping African countries use them to develop their agricultural potential.'

It is true. Since the State of Israel came into being in 1948, the desert has bloomed. It is true, too, that given half a chance, some Arab states would wipe Israel off the map.

Sarah has been responsible for sending many scientists to Britain to talk about their work at Friends of Israel meetings. I go on to discuss with her the kind of speakers we would like for next year. I shake hands with her, leave the building and walk onto a busy street where I find a café. I buy coffee and a piece of quiche.

An hour later I am outside Notre Dame, a Roman Catholic conference house, boarding a bus bound for a refugee camp in the West Bank. The trip has been organised by Stephen, the General Secretary of a large Christian organisation. There are a dozen of us – including six German Lutheran pastors, an American Methodist minister called David Franks, Joyce Pearson who is a writer from Cheshire. Next to me is Bill, an American Roman Catholic priest working at the Peace and Justice Commission of the Vatican.

Later that afternoon, we are piling out of the bus outside the camp. It is surrounded by a fence 12 or 15 feet high. At this point, there is pedestrian access only through a turnstile. As we are about to go through the turnstile, Stephen explains to us that there is only one other pedestrian entrance and one vehicular one. He goes on to explain that the camp is one square kilometre, but has 9,000 inhabitants, most of whom live in single storey buildings. Sixty-five per cent of the 750,000 population of the West Bank live in camps. This compares with 30 per cent of the 900,000 inhabitants of the Gaza Strip who are in camps.

As we are going through the turnstile we are greeted by Rashid, a social worker employed by the United Nations. He was born in this camp and still lives here. We follow him along narrow alleys between concrete houses, and then we stop outside one of them. Children are playing on the step. Rashid explains that sometimes the military authorities declare a round-the-clock curfew for days on end, preventing shopping, work, education and medical treatment. There is freedom of movement for only two hours a day when people have to get water and do their shopping. Punishment for breaking the curfew varies between imprisonment and being shot. As we walk on, I notice that Rashid is limping.

We arrive at his house and meet his wife and children.

They are a beautiful and charming family. The lounge is comfortable, westernised and beautifully kept. Twelve of us sit down and ask Rashid questions.

'What is medical care like in the refugee camp and in the West Bank?' I ask.

'There is only one children's hospital for the whole of the West Bank. There is only one doctor for this refugee camp. Medical treatment is a problem. We can't afford to pay for the better Israeli hospitals.'

'Palestinians are generally very well educated. Does this reflect a good educational system in the West Bank?'

'On the contrary there are a number of fields of study which are forbidden in the West Bank universities. For example, there is no Medical School.' There is machine gun fire outside, not many yards away. Everyone except Rashid and his family ducks or flinches.

'What's that?'

'It's the military shooting at someone. It happens all the time. As I was saying, there is the University of Bethlehem, but with restricted fields of study. There is no political opportunity for us in the West Bank and no economy so we try hard to get education in spite of the difficulties. Even so, the highest numbers of highly-qualified Palestinians are from the following, in order of percentage: cities, villages and refugee camps. It is very difficult for us here in these camps. The Israeli Government would rather give a permit for a person to study abroad than have them stay, but we can get exit permits for only three years. After that, we must return and have them renewed. This is risky when people are doing a four-year or five-year degree course in Germany, for example. I have known some students come back only to find that they are not allowed to return, having used up the family resources and therefore having to work as labourers. This means that many students are frightened to return, in case their permits are not renewed. They end up staying overseas which is precisely what the Israelis want. They are bleeding this country of the people who were born here.'

'We have heard that permits are required for very many things in the West Bank. Can you explain?'

'It is rare, for example, for permits to be given for us to bring in machinery for industry. This is preventing our economy from getting off the ground. We need permits before we can plant fruit trees. In practice, very few permits are given – of course, the Israelis can point to Palestinians who have been given permits and they use that as a propaganda exercise. For most of us, permits are hard to come by. Also, the military authorities often use permits to bribe Palestinians into collaboration.'

'Can you tell us about Palestinian land rights?' we ask.

Rashid smiles. 'We are supposed to have rights, but in practice, if the Israelis want to take Palestinian land then they take it. We are supposed to be protected by law, but it's amazing how there seems to be one law for us and one for the Jews.' At this point orange juice is brought, in spite of the fact that our hosts are keeping Ramadan and cannot partake of it themselves.

'What are relations like between ordinary Palestinians and the military?'

'There are some good soldiers and some bad ones, but the problem is that we have little means of complaining against the bad ones. For example, it is now Ramadan. Some friends of mine had just prepared the food. The signal had come from the Mosque to say that the fast was over and that they could eat when soldiers walked in, saw them sitting down to their meal and just knocked the food and drink all over the floor. Sometimes the soldiers are ordered to act brutally. When a Palestinian is arrested for a serious offence, his wife and children are evicted from their house, and then it is blown up or bulldozed.

'In December, I was sitting in a friend's car outside the camp. By the side of the road there was a Jewish settler talking to two Israeli soldiers. He was carrying a machine pistol. For no reason, he walked over to the car and fired a burst of rounds through the window. Three rounds went into my legs. My friend got out of the car and shouted to the soldiers to help. They just lifted their hands and walked off. I have tried to have the man arrested, but failed. I know who he is, but I am not listened to.'

'Are many people in prison, and what things are people put in prison for?'

'There are people in prison for terrorist offences and so-called terrorist offences. There are women in prison for writing slogans and distributing leaflets. There are even 12 and 13-year-olds in detention. Children who throw stones are sometimes arrested. Every family knows someone who has been imprisoned – I have been in prison 11 times for doing no more than my job as a social worker.'

We walk back to the turnstile along the narrow alleys, while little boys run out of their houses to touch us or to shake our hands. When we are approaching the turnstile, we see two soldiers fiddling with their guns. I look at Rashid and wonder what price he will have to pay for giving us hospitality.

Not far from the camp, we see a civilian standing on the pavement with a machine pistol resting on his arm. A few yards from him are some Israeli soldiers.

As planned, we arrive at a church boarding school in a small West Bank town. While we are waiting in a lounge for the head teacher, one of the staff answers some more of our questions. 'The West Bank and Gaza are run by military edict. Military edicts, for example, declare that not more than ten people can gather for anything which might be perceived to be political. This rules out Palestinian dancing. Our culture is being destroyed.

'In 1948, many Palestinians left their houses in what is now Israel in fear, expecting to return in a week or two. They and their children are still in refugee camps, their homes having been appropriated.'

The head teacher, a little man in his fifties, then comes

into the room. After apologising for keeping us waiting, he goes on to tell us about his school and the denomination to which it belongs.

'This is a boarding school. We only take children if they are orphans, neglected or rejected. It is strange therefore that we were closed down by military order from December 1987 until August 1988. I am a refugee. My family were millionaires back in 1948. All our property was taken then. My parents took me and fled on hearing of a massacre in a neighbouring village. We were not allowed to return. Other refugees couldn't prove ownership of their own property and so were evicted.

'In 1980, my uncle won his case in court and was given ownership of his own house, but then he was presented with a bill for repairs and for the rates since 1948. This was more than the value of the house, so it was taken from him. We have lost everything except our dignity.

'The government is trying to suppress education. Regarding the school curriculum, history has been rewritten. Not all subjects are allowed to be taught at university level. Most schools don't have laboratories or the right equipment. West Bank teachers earn 600 shekels a month, whereas Israeli teachers earn 2,000 to 3,000 shekels. Teachers are often forced to teach subjects about which they know nothing. Every so often (the last time was one and a half years ago) schools are closed for days, weeks or even months. There have been military orders preventing teachers and pupils from carrying textbooks or exercise books. Teachers were prevented from teaching in their own homes under threat of imprisonment. During close-downs teachers' pay is cut by 25 per cent, even though they want to work. The West Bank is said to be under civil administration. This is a euphemism. It is the military who govern.

'There is no friction between Christians and Muslims in Palestine. Everywhere you see a mosque, you see a church next to it. We have lived side-by-side for 1,400 years. Before the State of Israel, we lived happily with the Jews, too.

'There are cases of unarmed civilians being killed by the military in their own homes, and then their houses demolished. This happened to a friend of mine back in 1983. He was sitting at home with his wife, went to the front door and was gunned down by the military. His wife was then given five minutes to get the children out of the house before it was demolished.'

We are then taken on a tour of the school before jumping back on the bus. I am sad at first and then angry. I do not care any more if they throw stones at my car. If I were them I would do more than throw stones.

With an hour of daylight left, I drive to the Mount of Olives to chat to Mike and Bassam. I tell them that I now understand. 'You know', says Mike. 'My house is very small and we are overcrowded. I want to make it bigger. There is no problem, because there is land behind the house, but I have been refused a permit to build an extension. Israelis can get permits to make their houses bigger, but we can't. For those of us who don't have land or a house, the situation is even more difficult.'

Anyone predicting that in six months the Israelis and the PLO will sign a peace accord would be scorned. Even if the miracle of peace comes, it will take an even bigger miracle to heal the wounds of oppression and conflict.

I walk a few yards from Mike and Bassam and look over the parapet. Ten feet below is the grave of Robert Maxwell. The grave is dug in land that was once Palestinian. In it lies a man who was neither Israeli nor Palestinian, but whose family could afford to pay an 'undisclosed' price. I lean on the parapet and look out at Jerusalem over the Kidron Valley. I want to weep.

The next day, I am in West Jerusalem enjoying a Sabbath meal at the home of Reuven and Naomi, a retired Israeli couple. Reuven was born and brought up in Salford, two miles from my church. Round the table are six others, all Israeli except Olivia, a Methodist from Redditch, and Alphonse, an American clergyman. Prayers are said and then white wine is poured. Reuven proudly tells us that this wine was grown on the Golan Heights. The vineyards had been planted soon after the Israeli occupation of that region in 1967. I wince and think of the Syrians who once owned that land. Alphonse, the American clergyman, lifts his glass and says, 'And long may they keep their vineyards!' There are murmurs of agreement from everyone except me, and Olivia from Redditch.

She asks, 'What do you mean?'

'Giving back the Golan to the Syrians could be part of the deal worked out in the peace process', replies Alphonse.

'It is important for us to keep those vineyards', says a voice from across the table. Olivia is flabbergasted.

'What? More important than peace?' she asks.

'It is not easy for us to convey what this land means to us', says Reuven. 'This is the land given to Abraham thousands of years ago. For 2,000 years Jews were pushed from pillar to post, and then there was the Holocaust. I was in the Royal Air Force during the war, but when I was demobbed I came out here. We couldn't expect the survivors from the concentration camps to build this nation. They were too sick. I have helped to build this country. When we came here, it was a desert. If it had been left to the Arabs it would still be a desert. We are now one of the most civilised countries in the world. And furthermore, Jews will never again be pushed around. Whenever they are persecuted, wherever they are in the world, they know that they have a home here.'

'It's not civilised the way that Israel treats people in Gaza', says Olivia.

'You don't know these Arabs! They support hijacking and terrorism! The Arabs hate each other. And besides, they support Saddam Hussein. There are 27 Arab nations and only one Jewish one. We are surrounded by enemies. These people in the Gaza, why do they have to live there? Why can't Jordan, Egypt, Syria or Iraq take them?'

'But they were born in Palestine.'

'This land was given to our ancestors! Having said that, I must tell you that our government is generous to the Arabs. We have offered a home to 70 Muslims from Bosnia. You know, the Palestinians accused us of doing it as a publicity stunt.'

I drive back to St George's disturbed. Zionism is a beautiful ideal: God giving a land to the people he loves, that they may live in peace and plenty. But, they tell me that part of what has been given to one people has been taken from another.

Next morning, I am still disturbed, so I go for a long walk into the old walled city of Jerusalem. Just before I enter the Damascus gate I overhear two German tourists. 'We must not go into the old city. It is too dangerous.' On hearing this misconception, I feel sorrow and anger. I want to walk and walk to get the churned-up feelings out of my system. As I pass up and down the narrow alleys, I am struck that there are so few people about. The crowds were swelled yesterday by Friday prayers. As I pass by the empty bazaars, I am encouraged to step inside and browse. I explain that I don't have much money, but I talk to them about the Israeli occupation of the old city. I hear the same story time and again: 'Our trade is being ruined.'

I walk down a narrow passage that leads from the old city. Just before I emerge from it into the square in front of the Western Wall, I see three armed Israeli soldiers leaning against the wall. 'Shalom', I say. 'Shalom', they reply. I want to chat, so, though I am not lost, I ask the way. I tell them that I am from England and am finding it hard to get my bearings. Moments later I am talking to one of them about Manchester United football club. He looks Ethiopian and is the only one with much English. 'How long have you been in Israel?' I ask.

'Nearly two years. I'm from Ethiopia. I was a school teacher, until four years ago. My school was blown up in the fighting. I ran away and nearly died of starvation. Many people are persecuted but it is worse for Jews. I lived in a refugee camp in Addis for a year until the Israelis flew me out on 16 May 1991. It was the happiest day of my life. My friends here', he says, pointing to his comrades, 'think that Israel is a country under siege. They think it's tough here. I don't fear Saddam Hussein. I don't fear Assad. I don't fear the PLO. I don't fear Ayatollahs. There were people like them in the Bible but we Israelis defeated them. God gave us strength. He will do it again. I tell you, in spite of threats from outside, this country is a place of shalom. It is a place of safety for God's people. There is food and money. We have clean water and places to live. This is paradise. The Israeli government is the most generous on earth.'

In the afternoon, I go back to St George's Cathedral. It is surrounded by a high wall and huge steel gates. I press the buzzer and say who I am. The gates roll back. I have an appointment with a certain Palestinian canon. When I tell him that I am the chairman of a Friends of Israel Association, he looks uncomfortable. Palestinians find it hard to believe that a person of integrity could hold such a post. I sit in his study, apologetic and nervous. 'In Britain, Jews are discriminated against. They need friends. And as long as I am a friend I can try to build bridges.'

He smiles and leans back in his chair. 'You can try to build bridges and you might succeed, but I can tell you that once you show that you are campaigning for Palestinians, you will lose your friends. I hope you don't lose them, but I think you will.'

I have been invited to the home of Klaus and Ruth Schindler in a quiet suburb of West Jerusalem for coffee and cakes. Ruth answers the door and welcomes me as if I were her son returning from the war. She is effusive. 'Mr Howard, it is so good to meet you. To think, the chairman of the Friends of Israel is in our humble home.'

'Mrs Schindler, the honour is mine. And, please, call me

Geoff.' She takes me into her sitting room and introduces me to her husband, a frail man in his eighties. He remains seated in his armchair while I shake his hand.

'Forgive me for not rising to my feet. My legs don't work very well', he says in a strong accent. I sit in an armchair next to him. We chat about life in Britain and the role of the Friends of Israel. I drink two cups of coffee and eat more pastries than I would normally allow myself. Klaus questions me about the rise of neo-fascism in Western Europe and wants to know whether it is a real threat. 'Fascism in the thirties and forties was the greatest evil this world has ever seen. I am the only member of my family to survive. My mother and father, two sisters, my brother, my first wife and daughter died in death camps. I was almost dead when the Americans came and liberated us.

'There was no way I could have lived in Germany any more. There were many good people in Germany at the time of Hitler, but they were powerless. The only way for Jewish people to be safe was for us to have a nation of our own. The State of Israel exists to ensure that there will never again be another Holocaust. Wherever our people are persecuted, they know that they have a safe home here.

'The Palestinians resent our being here. They have been our enemy since the time of David and Goliath. History repeats itself. You watch – David will slay the giant once more and then our people will truly be free to live in peace.'

Monday 1 March, and I am back on the Boeing 737, bound for Manchester. After breakfast, I recline the seat and try to sleep. I have been up since 4 a.m., but I can't stop thinking of the Palestinians I have met. They are decent people who ask for little. Mike would like an extension for his house. Rashid wants to live away from the refugee camp. I am unable to sleep, so I open the in-flight magazine. Of the 70 pages, eight are advertising property in Israel, enticing foreigners to buy a second home there. I think of people in the refugee camps who were born in what is now Israel. They would like one of these homes, but are prevented from living there.

The drinks trolley comes along and I buy a bottle of cream liqueur for my wife. When I put it in the locker above my head, I pick up the magazine again. It falls open at a picture of the old city of Jerusalem, photographed from the top of the Mount of Olives. It is a view I have come to know and love. I have looked at it for hours while chatting to Mike and Bassam, the postcard sellers. The scene is both moving and beautiful with the golden dome set among towers, churches and minarets. One cannot see the hurt of individuals from that spot, but the panorama is a symbol of the tension and pain that I have witnessed. Two mosques stand on the temple mount.

Jesus looks out from the Mount of Olives. There he sees the temple of Herod, the Antonia fortress, Herod's palace, a city teeming with thousands of inhabitants. He weeps. 'Jerusalem, Jerusalem, you that kill the prophets and stone those who are sent to you! How often have I longed to gather your children together, as a hen gathers her brood under her wings, and you refused!'

Later that week, as he is walking to his death, large numbers of people are following him. Among them are noblewomen who, as an act of charity, bring comfort to the condemned by making lament and offering them drugged wine. He is battered and bleeding, hardly able to put one foot in front of the other. The women are wailing because of him but he turns to them. 'Do not weep for me . . .'

Lord, my church needs its tower repairing. I have sickness in my family. I cry before you for them but, above all, I ask: remember Jerusalem.

9   Jesus Falls for the Third Time

> *Those who seek to get rid of me are powerful,*
> *my treacherous enemies. (Must I give back*
> *what I have never stolen?) Those who hope in*
> *you must not be made fools of, Yahweh*
> *Sabaoth, because of me! Those who seek you*
> *must not be disgraced, God of Israel, because*
> *of me. It is for you I bear insults, my face is*
> *covered with shame, I am estranged from my*
> *brothers, alienated from my own mother's*
> *sons; for I am eaten up with zeal for your*
> *house, and insults directed against you fall on*
> *me.*
>
> (Psalm 69:4; 6–9)

I have made another excursion to the West Bank and have been introduced to Da'ud, a Christian villager with a small farm. His family has lived on this land for many generations. Ten years ago, an official came and told him that his deed to the land and property was invalid. A few days later, the official returned with a group of men who began to cut down his olive trees and vines. Da'ud ran and brought a large number of friends. When the official's men saw that they were outnumbered, they fled, but not before more than half Da'ud's centuries-old trees and vines had been destroyed.

Da'ud went to church and asked that prayers be said for not only his land but also that of other villagers. A few months later, when he had planted more olive trees and vines, the government official returned. Da'ud was arrested for planting trees without a permit. When he was released a few months later, all the recently planted trees had been uprooted. He planted more. Since then, he has been in a legal battle with the civil administration. He is not yet defeated. 'I keep giving this problem to my Lord.' He prays for self-rule for the Palestinians, unaware that his is more than a vain hope.

I am in the church office listening to Edward, a 29-year-old. 'I've done something terrible.' He tells me of a weight round his neck that never allows him to walk tall. He is permanently depressed and often suicidal. I tell him that Christ, through the mystery of his passion, forgives and restores him. 'He carried your sin to the cross. He wants to free you from your burden by taking it upon himself. Give it to him.'

'I keep giving it to him but I keep on sinning. I don't want to. I'm driven. I loathe myself. I can't go on asking him to forgive me.'

'Jesus told Peter that he must forgive seventy-times-seven. If that was the standard for Peter, imagine what God's standard must be. He wants to free you from the cause of your sin. But if that freedom doesn't come straight away, you must go on giving him your sin. He will go on carrying it to the cross.'

I am in the home of Jenny and Peter on the sixteenth floor of a block of flats in my parish. I am at Jenny's bedside giving her communion. She is 52-years-old and has terminal cancer, with only a few days to live. Two years ago, the cancer was diagnosed. She took the problem to God and asked him to help her bear her burden. She was operated on. The consultant then told her that her chances were good. A year later, the cancer returned. Again she asked God to help her bear her burden. Radiotherapy appeared to have worked. Four months ago, secondary cancers were diagnosed. She says that were it not for God she would have despaired. As I am bringing her communion, she prays, 'Lord, you carried your cross for me. Help me to bear this one for you.' As she becomes weaker, she relies on his strength.

Reginald is a clergyman in the inner city. He and his wife Doreen have a baby girl and a three-year-old son. Recently, youths threw bricks through their window. The baby's cot was showered with glass. Their car has been vandalised. They have suffered two break-ins, one of them at night while Reginald was away. 'It is not easy to live here but God has called us. Without him we would not have the strength to carry on.'

Long after my grandfather retired, when I was 15, I started going to see him after school. Since his illness in 1953, he had fallen sick many times. We were so used to the medics saying that there was no hope that we never believed them. But, somehow, he staggered on. Time after time he fell sick. Time after time he pulled through. He was suffering from bronchitis and emphysema. When I used to go to see him at home, he was either in bed downstairs or sitting by the fire, but always fighting for breath. I often gave him a shave, cut his toenails and massaged his chest which was sore from coughing. As weak as he was, I still perceived him as being strong. It was he who sustained me and not I him.

When he had enough breath, I'd get him to tell me about his time in India or in the trenches. When he spoke, I could almost smell the cordite and hear the thunder of shells and the rumble of horse-drawn gun carriages. He told me of the heroism of others, but never of his own.

I had thought that I could rely on him forever. I had not thought that I could be strong unless he was strong, not stand unless he could stand. But I was learning that the weaker he was, the more I had to be strong.

The ugly procession moves on, the prisoner bent beneath the weight of his gallows. The cross that he carries is more than wood. It is Da'ud's struggle, Edward's sin, Jenny's sickness and the ministry of Reginald and Doreen. We all contribute to that weight. The world is on his shoulders. He has fallen twice and he is on the point of collapse again. He is no Atlas. He has emptied himself of any power to make this load light. 'For God's sake, don't fall', I want to say. 'If you go down, how can we stand? Be strong for us! Da'ud is relying on you. Reginald's ministry was crushing him until he gave it to you. Don't let it defeat you as well. If you fall there is no one strong enough to help us. You can't let the vandals and thieves beat you! You can't let Edward's sin get you down! Jenny's sickness must not afflict you! Bear your cross! If you fall, we will fall too!' At that, the prisoner hits the ground for the third time. It seems that hope is dead. The source of goodness in the world is near to defeat.

'Why are you so amazed at my weakness? You thought that because I am who I am, it's easy for me. Don't you understand, I can't bear sin and pain without cost to myself. This is no easy redemption. You don't suffer alone. I suffer with you and for you. If I were able to bear this without falling, then I would not be bearing it for real. Not even I can take the world's sin and pain and not be crushed by it. How could I walk with Auschwitz on my back and claim that the load is light enough to bear? You tell me to be strong so that you can be strong. Don't you understand that the reverse is true. I bear the cross so that you can be free from it. I fall so that you can stand.'

Lord, I have praised you for your greatness,

your splendour, your power and your majesty. Today, such praise is hollow. Any God can be great and powerful. Any God can elicit praise, but it is only you that can be weak for our sakes. We bow before you in your pain and humility.

10 Jesus is Stripped of His Clothes

*They took his clothing and divided it into four
shares, one for each soldier. His
undergarment was seamless, woven in one
piece from neck to hem; so they said one to
another, 'Instead of tearing it, let's throw dice
to decide who is to have it.' In this way the
words of scripture were fulfilled.*

(John 19:23–4)

John points and says, 'There's the lamb of God.'
Hearing this, Andrew is intrigued and follows the stranger.
He spends the day absorbed in his teaching. When it is time
to go home, he can't wait to tell his brother. 'I must go and
tell Peter! This is the most staggering news! God's kingdom
is here! I have found the Messiah! Neither I nor the world
will be the same again!' Andrew is so excited that he dashes
towards home through the dusty streets of Capernaum. He
holds onto his head-wrap as he flies round a corner, where
he bumps into a man wearing a sports jacket and a brown
plaid tie.

'What's the rush?' asks the man.

'I've got the most incredible news to tell my brother,
Peter. I want him to meet Jesus, the Messiah!'

'Ooooh, I wouldn't do that. Let me introduce myself. I'm
Mr Inter-Faith-Dialogue. You see, I know your Peter. He's
a Jew. It's dodgy telling a Jew about Jesus. You might offend
him.'

'Nah, not our Peter. Besides, it's fabulous news. It's
salvation!'

'Look, I'm involved in dialogue with the Jewish people.

We've been trying to gain their confidence for years. If you convert one of them it'll be a disaster, and we'll be back to square one.'

'Does that mean I can't tell Peter about Jesus?'

'Not directly. You'll cause offence. If he asks you, then it's all right, as long as you tell him that it's only your private opinion and that you think his religion is just as valid as yours.'

'Oh, well, I'm so excited that I'm sure he'll ask me and then I'll tell him, but', says Andrew, pausing for thought, 'I'll do as you say and let him know that his religion is as valid as mine.' With that Andrew rushes towards home.

Jesus, exhausted, allows the cross to fall. It hits the ground, bouncing as if in slow motion, making the hollow booming sound of heavy timber. He has reached Golgotha, bleeding and breathing heavily. Even without the cross, he can barely stand. The soldiers tell him to undress. He is too weak to undress himself, so they help, taunting him. The crowd turns tragedy into a bawdy spectacle. When Adam was naked, he took leaves to cover himself. The tree that Jesus has brought affords no leaves for covering. There is no shame quite like that of public nakedness.

Andrew, still in a hurry, rounds another corner and collides with a woman, knocking a pile of books out of her arms. He hurriedly picks them up for her, apologising.

'Slow down, young man, or you'll have a heart attack!'

'I'm sorry', says Andrew gasping for breath and gabbling his words. 'You see, I've found the Messiah. I'm off to tell my brother Peter.'

'Look, I'm Ms Liberal-Churchperson, and let me give you some advice. All this talk about finding the Messiah . . . well, Jews believe in Messiahs, but, you know, Jesus doesn't

talk in those terms. "Messiah" is a term to describe a mythical concept.'

'There's nothing mythical about Jesus!'

'Quite. He's just an ordinary man, conceived and born in
the same way as you and me, and with the same weak-
nesses. He's not mythical, but his Messiahship is. Let's face
it, God is never going to break into history, but we need the
idea of a Messiah to give us hope.'

'That's crazy! If God is never going to break into history
in a tangible way then we're deluding ourselves. If there's
no reality to back up the concept then our religion is gro-
tesque. It masks cruel realities just like opium.'

'Don't twist what I say. God is involved in history. He's
at work everywhere. The myth of the Messiah helps us to
understand that God is at work in the world.'

'I don't really understand you. Maybe Jesus isn't the
Messiah, but he's certainly worth listening to. I'm off to tell
Peter about him anyway.'

The soldiers stand back to let the crowd look
and make their ribald comments. Jesus is as naked as a man
in a shower, except that there is no curtain to hide him. He
is naked, prefiguring those six million people of his race
who were stripped for the gas chamber, stripped by soldiers
with a different uniform, a uniform bearing an emblem not
unlike a cross.

Andrew is almost home, but spots somebody
he met earlier when he was listening to the teaching of
Jesus. He goes over to him. At least this person will share
his enthusiasm. 'Brilliant news, eh! We've found the Messiah!' says Andrew.

The man goes purple, pressing his finger to his lips.
'Shhhh! Not so loud', he whispers. He continues in hushed
tones, on the look-out in case a passer-by should hear. 'Like

you, I believe in this Jesus. But I'm the Reverend Indirect-Approach. Your problem, Andrew, is that you're too enthusiastic. When you see Peter, you'll need to act cool. Don't overpower him, or else you'll make him feel uncomfortable. Don't use words like "God" or worse still "Jesus", that is not unless you're swearing.'

Andrew walks away with heavy feet, confused and unsure. Then, round the corner races Peter, wild with enthusiasm. 'Hey, Andrew, I hear that you've met that new preacher! What's he like?'

Andrew just groans. 'Don't bother to ask!'

> *Lord, when you healed the sick, pardoned the sinner and challenged corrupt authority, we saw God. When you taught and when you defeated evil forces, it was plain that you were divine. Everything you did had the mark of your father. But, in our cleverness, we have explained you away. We have diluted your teaching and made you a king without clothes. When Noah was seen naked by his son, Ham, it was not Noah who was cursed but Ham. Lord, in taking off your garment of divinity we bring no shame on you but on ourselves. And yet only as we look upon your shame, as you hang on the cross, do we find healing.*

11 Jesus is Nailed to the Cross

> *When they reached the place called The Skull,*
> *there they crucified him and the two*
> *criminals, one on his right the other on his*
> *left. Jesus said, 'Father, forgive them; they do*
> *not know what they are doing.' Then they cast*
> *lots to share out his clothing.*
>
> (Luke 23:33–4)

My first encounter with Dingas McGann occurs early in my first incumbency. I answer the door and he introduces himself. Standing with him is Mitch Smith. They are like a comedy act, bouncing jokes off each other and involving me in the repartee. Dingas has a bruise on his left cheek. 'You should have seen him', says Mitch. 'He took on three men in the Langworthy Pub and flattened the lot of them.'

Dingas sticks his chest out and lifts his fists in a charade for boxing. 'No one can stand up to Dingas McGann', he says with a twinkle in his eye and looking sideways for approval from Mitch. 'Anyway', he adds, dropping his fists, 'can we earn a few bob by doing a couple of hours work in your garden?'

I agree, give them the tools and go back to my desk. Fifteen minutes pass and they come back to the door, asking for payment. Dingas argues that he has been working for more than two hours. His jovial manner has gone and he is aggressive. I wonder if I am in physical danger. In the end I cut my losses and give them a small payment and tell them to go. They go away mumbling threats.

For the next couple of years I do not see much of Mitch,

though Dingas calls perhaps once a month for a sandwich and a cup of tea. When I am feeling generous, I give him a little money. His conversation is usually about the fights he has been in. On one occasion he says, 'I was jumped on again. This time there were five of them. They tried to take my money. I put one of them in hospital. The others ran off to nurse their wounds. No one tangles with Dingas McGann and gets away with it!' There is pleasure in his voice. He then asks me for £5. When I give him 50p and a sandwich, he turns his anger on me. I shut the door.

Then, one Saturday, I am walking out of the vicarage to go to my church's summer fair. Coming in through the gate is Dingas McGann. He asks for a sandwich and a cup of tea. I explain that the summer fair has already started and that I am in a hurry to get there. I invite him to come with me, and tell him I'll buy him a meal when we get there.

When we get to the church, he stays outside, asking me to bring the food out to him. As I walk towards the snack bar, I am stopped by several people who want a word with me. Dingas McGann is still outside and becoming impatient. After ten minutes, when I am standing at the counter placing his order, he storms in. The hall is noisy and packed. He has to squeeze between people to get to me. When he has done so, he clears his throat and shouts loudly, 'This man isn't fit to be your vicar. He refused to give a thirsty man a drink of water!' I am flabbergasted at this fabrication.

Everyone within ten yards of him hears. His lie needles me. He is about to shout something else out and I am powerless to stop him. In the heat of the moment I am unable to see the situation clearly. I imagine that everyone will believe him. My name will be tainted forever.

I whisper loudly in his ear saying that if he knows what is good for him he will keep his mouth shut. He takes this as a threat and says, 'Right, we'll settle this outside.' Here is a chance to get him out of the building and prevent him from spreading any more lies about me. I push past people in the hall and make for the door.

I am so scared that I feel ill. I will be severely injured. His method of fighting is well known. If he knocks me to the ground, there will be no count of ten. He'll kick me mercilessly. Internal injuries, broken bones, blood, disfigurement seem inevitable. I might die. The thought of how anyone could hurt me for such a distorted motive is beyond me. I was in the act of feeding a hungry man when I was blamed for something I did not do. Now I'm being punished for it. Jesus fed the hungry, too. And it was lies that nailed him to the cross.

The soldiers drag him to the ground and stretch him out. They kneel on him, holding his arm along the cross-member, disregarding the agony on his face. A mallet drives home the metal spike. Those who had asked for blood look on. 'We could not be safe with him around. It's either him or us.'

I push my way onto the street ahead of Dingas. My back is to him but I sense him on my heels. He speaks, telling me that I'm about to meet my end. He is going to hit me from behind. I am gripped with terror. Is this how Jesus felt as they were about to drive home those nails? How could anyone injure another? I'm terrified. I think, 'It's him or me!' I explode, spin on my heel and throw my body behind my fist. There is a crunch as it hits him between the eyes. In microseconds I reason, 'I've hurt him. He'll be so enraged that he'll kill me! I've got to hurt him so badly that he won't be able to get me.' The first punch has barely landed when I follow it with more and a head butt. He is now falling as my knee rises to catch him brutally on the head.

Dingas hits the ground, his mouth and nose bleeding. He

is lying almost still, groaning. I stand over him breathing heavily. I look at Jesus lying there.

> *I wondered why they wanted to hurt you and why Dingas wanted to hurt me? Now I know. I am ashamed to say it but, if you had been a threat to me as you were to the Pharisees, I would have nailed you to the tree. Lord have mercy.*

12 Jesus Dies

*From the sixth hour there was darkness over
all the land until the ninth hour. And about
the ninth hour, Jesus cried out in a loud voice,
'Eli, eli, lama sabachthani?' that is, 'My God,
my God, why have you forsaken me?' When
some of those who stood there heard this,
they said, 'The man is calling on Elijah,' and
one of them quickly ran to get a sponge which
he filled with vinegar and, putting it on a reed,
gave it to him to drink. But the rest of them
said, 'Wait! And see if Elijah will come to save
him.' But Jesus, again crying out in a loud
voice, yielded up his spirit. And suddenly, the
veil of the Sanctuary was torn in two from
top to bottom, the earth quaked, the rocks
were split, the tombs opened and the bodies
of many holy people rose from the dead.*

(Matthew 27:45–52)

It is 4:30 p.m., a day early in February 1963,
three weeks before my eighteenth birthday. I am walking
down my street on my way home from school, filled with
dread. In the last year, grandfather has been critically ill in
hospital four times. He is ill again but his doctor has refused
to have him admitted; nothing more can be done. I called
in to see him this morning and wondered whether I would
ever see him again. As I walk down the street, I know that
if his front room curtains are closed, he has died. I approach
the house not daring to look.

Day after day, I come home from school and the pattern

is the same. I am filled with dread as I approach the house and am then relieved when I see the curtains open. Each night, members of the family take it in turn to sit up with him. I volunteer to take Saturday nights. There is no school in the morning, and though I do not admit it, it is an opportunity to be in bed legitimately during boring church services next morning. In all my grandfather's weakness, he is still a strength to me.

He has been kept up all night, flogged and beaten. His scalp has been lacerated. He has carried timber weighing heavier than a man for half a mile. Spikes have been driven through him and now the weight of his torn and tortured flesh hangs from them. If a dog suffered half as much, we would shoot it. We stand there helpless, thinking a blasphemy. We wish his suffering were over; we want him to die. He would have made a great leader. We had dreams for him but they were not to be. It is best that he goes quickly now. Then, with a loud cry he dies and so does his suffering. When we die our suffering dies with us. When he died, he freed everyone from the form of life that endures suffering.

Saturday 24 February, two days after my eighteenth birthday, it is my turn to sit up with grandfather all night. He is in bed in the back room downstairs. A fire is burning in the grate. On the floor is a bed bottle and a spittoon – a bucket with disinfectant in the bottom. He is sitting up against a pile of pillows struggling to breathe. It is 11:30 p.m. and grandmother has gone to bed. 'How d'you feel granddad?' I ask softly, but he will not complain.

I bring in a shovel of coal, and settle beside him in a chair to do my maths homework. The slightest noise is a distraction. The clock is ticking, the coal hissing in the grate, and grandfather gasping. Every few minutes, I attend to him. I lift him when he has slid down the pillows or give him a drink or the bed bottle.

He is gasping for his life. He had cheerfully returned to the front after being wounded, but now he cries out, 'I don't want to die' – the cry he heard from the trenches. I help him to a drink of lemon and barley water from a feeder cup, and give him a bed bottle. At 1:30 a.m. he has not enough breath to speak. His eyes are half-open, and his jaw gaping. His chest is rising and falling violently 80 times a minute. I pray as his snatching for breath becomes slower, punctuated by silent pauses. Each gasp is distinct from the rest. He is breathing deeply and noisily, as if in anger, with the rhythm of a bicycle pump. At two o'clock, he is gasping twelve times a minute. At three o'clock there is a loud and violent breath four times a minute. For seconds, he lies as if dead and then his chest heaves with a mighty gasp. I touch him on the shoulder but there is no response. There will be no more stories of India from this old soldier. It is no use calling the doctor. He has told us not to bother him; there is nothing he can do.

I open the door into the hall and climb the stairs. Grandmother is awake. 'He hasn't got long', I say. 'I'm going across the road to get mum and dad. I'll be back in a minute.' Moments later I return. Grandma is holding his hand. 'George, are you all right?' she asks. Then, my mother walks in. We can hear the clock ticking and the coal hissing in the grate. He has been ailing for years. He is now taking his rest. I have seen grandfather suffer for years. For selfish reasons I have wanted him to hang on. I had dreams that we would get some more out of life together, but that is not to be. It is best for him that he goes quickly. Then with a loud cry, he dies.

As the Boeing 737 touches down on 1 March in a blizzard at Manchester Airport, I know that I can be silent no longer. I will have to open my mouth, but I deeply regret the hurt this will cause in the Jewish community. No matter what I say or how I say it, it will cause pain. If only I could see the progress made in the Palestinian peace talks, it would make things easier for me.

I arrive home exhausted, having been up most of the night but the first thing I do is try to telephone my Jewish friend, Sir Sidney Hamburger. I am chairman and he is president of the North-West Friends of Israel Association. He is not in his office. I am relieved as I do not feel like having a confrontation. Instead of trying again to 'phone him I write to him, telling him of some of the things I have experienced in Israel and the West Bank. I tell him that I am in an awkward position. I do not wish to cause the Friends of Israel embarrassment. On the other hand I cannot be silent. I request a meeting with him.

A few days later I have not heard from him so I ring him. Yes, he will happily meet me but not yet. He is going away for a few weeks. Instead, he suggests that I meet the Israeli Embassy press attaché when he comes to Manchester.

Before he goes away, he writes to me, enclosing a newspaper cutting reporting that a Muslim fundamentalist had killed a tourist in Egypt. In the letter, he tells me of atrocities in Israel perpetrated by Palestinians. He is trying to counter my experiences.

A week later, I still have not had a meeting with Sir Sidney but I am speaking on the phone to another Jewish friend. I make a casual remark about a Friends of Israel meeting scheduled for November. 'But I thought that it was cancelled, I understood that . . . that . . .' he stammers. Then he starts to waffle. I am reading between the lines. It is dawning on me that perhaps the meeting has been cancelled because of the embarrassment at having me, a 'pro-Palestinian', as chairman.

I conclude that the sentence has been passed and that my chairmanship will be terminated. I might be able to speak out for the Palestinians but I will no longer have either credibility or an audience. I want to hang on to the chairmanship. I had dreams that I would be able to build bridges but it appears that will not be possible. As far as this post is concerned, I am a dead man. At least when I am gone, there will be less pain all round.

September 1990. I have been in the same inner-city parish for more than 13 years. Early in my ministry here, I saw the congregation grow in faith and in numbers. A handful of young families joined the church while at the same time we undertook ambitious improvements on the building. But, after 13 years, I have become tired. Numbers are dropping and I do not have the vision I had. My ministry here is in the final stages of decay. It is better to let it die rather than cling onto it. I had dreams for this parish but they were not to be. It is best that I go quickly. I write to the bishop to tell him that I am ready for a move.

> *Lord, you made us to live. Even so, death is a blessing that brings an end to decay and opens the way to life.*

13 Jesus is Taken Down from the Cross

Now in Jerusalem there was a man named Simeon. He was an upright and devout man; he looked forward to the restoration of Israel and the Holy Spirit rested on him. It had been revealed to him by the Holy Spirit that he would not see death until he had set eyes on the Christ of the Lord. Promoted by the Spirit he came to the Temple; and when the parents brought in the child Jesus to do for him what the Law required, he took him into his arms and blessed God ... As the child's father and mother were wondering at the things that were being said about him, Simeon blessed them and said to Mary his mother, 'Look, he is destined for the fall and the rise of many in Israel, destined to be a sign that is opposed — and a sword will pierce your soul too — so that the secret thoughts of many may be laid bare.'

(Luke 2:25–7; 33–5)

I feel no less close to grandfather than when he was alive. It is hard to believe that he is a corpse while the warmth of life is still in him. I put in his false teeth, take off his pyjamas and help to wash his body. It is no less an act of love than helping him with the feeder cup. By now my father and uncle have arrived. My father and I take hold of his legs and my uncle Bert his arms. We carry him naked into the front room, and lay him on the couch.

I have been sad but at peace. But then my thoughts become disturbed. The doctor told us not to bother him. There was nothing he could do. Why had I believed him? At midnight, why had I not sprinted to a telephone box and phoned for an ambulance? In spite of what the doctor said, I know that if grandfather had been admitted to hospital he would have come round. 'Granddad, forgive me for watching you suffer and doing nothing about it. I blame myself.'

A soldier, making sure that Jesus is dead, thrusts a lance into his side. The man from Arimathaea is looking on. With only three hours before sunset and the Shabbatt, he runs and requests an audience with Pilate to ask for the body. Pilate confirms with the centurion that the prisoner is dead and gives the Arimathaean leave to take the corpse. With no time to lose, he buys a shroud and goes back to the site of the crucifixion. The prisoner has been hanging dead for some time. John, Mary and her friends are waiting there. With John and a soldier to help, the Arimathaean removes the nails and lowers the prisoner to the ground, where his mother takes his head and cradles it in her arms. She uses her garment to wipe the dried blood from his face and then kisses him as her tears fall on him.

'I had such hopes for you. What kind of glory is this?' she asks. 'Water into wine, raising the dead, teaching the multitudes. That's glory! My son, what have you done? You have gone too far. You have challenged the wrong people. Why couldn't you have stayed in Galilee? Why couldn't you have been more careful? Would it have mattered if you'd waited until the Sabbath to heal the sick? Why did you call people "vipers" and "whitewashed tombs"? No wonder they opposed you. If you had been a little more tactful you would have gone on using your marvellous talents until you were an old man. What purpose does this serve? What a waste of your gifts! I had such hopes.

'Things might have been different if I had not been ambitious for you. It was I who started this. It was I who forced your hand at Cana. I wanted to see your glory but I didn't know it would come to this!'

> *Lord, I blame myself for things over which I have no control but do not admit my failures. Give me a right judgement in all things.*

14   Jesus is Laid in the Tomb

*It was now evening, and since it was
Preparation Day – that is, the day before the
Sabbath – there came Joseph of Arimathaea, a
prominent member of the Council, who
himself lived in the hope of seeing the kingdom
of God, and he boldly went to Pilate and
asked for the body of Jesus. Pilate, astonished
that he should have died so soon, summoned
the centurion and enquired if he had been dead
for some time. Having been assured of this
by the centurion, he granted the corpse to
Joseph who bought a shroud, took Jesus
down from the cross, wrapped him in the
shroud and laid him in a tomb which had
been hewn out of the rock. He then rolled a
stone against the entrance to the tomb. Mary
of Magdala and Mary the mother of Joset took
note of where he was laid.*

(Mark 15:42–7)

It is 1980 and I am officiating at the funeral of a
76-year-old woman. A few days later, I go to see her sister,
Maud, a woman in her late sixties. I sit on her settee listening to her. 'I am all alone now. My husband died five years
ago. I have no children. No relatives at all.'

'Not even any cousins?'

'No one.' From that time, Maud becomes a member of
my church. Each Christmas she comes to my home for
lunch. The children love her. She is an extra grandmother.
She helps with the preparation of the meal, plays with

the young ones and helps with the washing-up. As each Christmas draws near, it is understood that she will come. She never needs to ask; we never need to invite. She is always welcome.

It is 1991, and my church is rehearsing *The Six Wives of Henry VIII*. My wife has a leading part. Rehearsals drag on and are then suspended because of casting problems. Before rehearsals resume, I announce that I am moving to another parish. The move is a strange one. The bishop has asked me to go to the neighbouring parish, only a short walk away. I have visions of half the congregation moving with me. Painful though it is, I tell my congregation that they must not follow me. I joke with them saying that if I see any one of them in the pew at my new church, I will point and ask the person to leave. I cannot allow any exceptions. One special case will lead to another.

I move just after Easter. A short while later, the producer of *The Six Wives of Henry VIII* rings up and asks me to inform my wife that rehearsals are starting again. 'I'm sorry, Terry', I say. 'She's not going to be in the play. We've moved parish now. We have to leave a clear field for the new man.'

Terry is devastated. He tells me that she is perfect for the part and irreplaceable. The play will be ruined. He cannot understand my reasoning. I tell him that unless we are out of the picture, we will distort future ministry in that parish. He pleads with me, telling me that the play should be an exception. Everyone will understand, he claims. My emotions are with him. I want to relent but I know that to do so would burst the dam.

A few days later the undertaker rings me with a funeral from my former parish. 'I'm sorry', I say, 'I'm no longer at St Ambrose's.'

'I know', he says, 'but the family have requested you.'

'I'm sorry', I say. 'You must ask someone else.' I put down the 'phone, wounded by my own callousness.

As Christmas approaches, my old parish is still in inter-regnum. Maud is on my mind. I have neither seen her nor visited her since the move, even though she lives only five minutes walk from my new house. I have enquired about her and know that people from the church are visiting her but I have not been in contact. If I invite her to lunch at Christmas, the others might ask why she is a special case. I have had to be unyielding for the sake of the unity of the parish we have just left.

So, Maud cannot come to lunch. The local Methodist church is putting on a lunch on Christmas Day. Maud lives only 150 yards from it. On some Sunday evenings she worships there and knows the congregation. I ring the min-ister and arrange for her to be invited. When the invitation is sent to her she declines. 'I'm having lunch at Geoff's', she says. 'I always have lunch at Geoff's.' I go to see her. I sit drinking tea out of a china cup and eating digestive biscuits. I explain that we are unable to invite her this year. She looks shocked and goes pale.

'Are you all right, Maud?'

'I'm all right', she says. 'I quite understand.' But I know that she is not all right and that she does not understand. My ministry in the other parish is finished. A little fruit might continue but the ministry itself is no more. It died the day I moved. There are those who deny its death. They want to hang on to the corpse in the hope that one day it will come alive. The only thing to do is bury it and leave it buried. Otherwise the new ministry cannot begin.

The Arimathaean, helped by the soldiers, and followed by two of the women, carries the stretcher to the tomb. There is no life in Jesus. His ministry is finished but the women cannot come to terms with it. They want to hang on to the corpse. The only thing to do is bury it and leave it buried. Otherwise the new ministry cannot begin. Jesus is placed in the tomb in haste, before the onset of darkness. The women do not want to leave him entombed. They know that they must return with spices. They cannot allow decomposition. They cannot let this grain of wheat go.

I am helping to carry my grandfather's coffin into the crematorium. He carried me when I was young and now I carry him. It is what love demands. I feel inseparable from him. Though dead, his physical presence is still sustaining me. We lower the coffin onto the catafalque and walk to a pew. I do not hear a word of the service. At the end, I get up and, in a daze, step forward to take the coffin home. I realise what I am doing and burst into tears. I must leave this old soldier here and go on my way. I cannot hang on to him.

Life is not going to be the same. In letting go of him I must stand on my own feet now, but one thing I know, I am the better able to do it for having known him.

The body is in the tomb. Then the sun sets, ushering in the Shabbatt. The eleven are in the room together. For hours they have been going over the events, playing the 'if only' game. 'We should have stopped him from coming to Jerusalem.'

'We tried but he wouldn't listen. He knew what was going to happen. He walked straight into it.'

'Right up to the end I thought he'd get out of it. On every other occasion, he's outwitted them.'

'D'you remember that first time he took us to the synagogue?'

'When that strange man kept shouting out?'

'Yeah, but he soon silenced him. And then afterwards we invited him back for a bite to eat. It was embarrassing when the mother-in-law was too ill to get the meal ready. There was no fuss though. He just said a quick prayer over her. Up she got and fixed the supper.'

'The way he handled the lawyers was brilliant. They used to run rings round us but he always made them look silly. I could go anywhere with him. The fanatics didn't frighten me when he was around.'

'Nor did the military.'

'D'you remember that day when all those people followed us round the lake? He said, "You live round here. Where can we get some bread?" I thought he was winding me up. My village was three miles away. It was a joke. I couldn't exactly go to the baker and say, "Five thousand loaves. And . . . could you lend me half a dozen ox carts to carry them?" '

'What got me was the way he knew more about my job than I did. I used to wonder what a joiner from Nazareth could know about the lake. Until he came here, the biggest stretch of water he'd seen was at the bottom of a well. When he told us to fish in daylight when we'd been up all night, I almost swore at him. I wanted my bed.'

'And d'you remember when we were shipping water in that squall? We were rowing for our lives and he was having a doze. I woke him and gave him a bucket to bail us out. He was furious.'

'It didn't matter where we were, we were always safe.'

'Look at us now. Every knock on the door and we jump out of our skins. I'm terrified at the thought of going out to buy bread or bring water. When it's my turn, I'll pull my hood forward, and run, looking at the ground.'

'If only he hadn't been so stupid as to get himself killed.'

'He had such high hopes for us. He said we'd do greater things than he did. Some hope!'

'I'm terrified to go out the front door. And even when things blow over, I couldn't go back to that way of life. I can't make a speech at a wedding let alone preach.'

'And as for healing the sick, d'you remember that day

when the three of you had gone with him up Mount Tabor? They brought a sick child to us. I told his father that we'd make him well. Two hours later the kid was nearly dead, writhing on the ground.'

'There's no way that we'll ever turn out as he wanted us to. If he'd lived, it would have been different. I'm not cut out for fishing for men. I'm going back to my nets.'

Postscript

I did not want to resign my chairmanship of the North-West Friends of Israel Association, but I felt that it might cause the Jewish community less pain than if I were to continue. But, I decided to wait until after my meeting with the Israeli Embassy press attaché before coming to a decision. As the meeting drew near, I was dreading it. Whenever I have met with Israeli diplomatic staff, I have been impressed by their skill. Their charm and grasp of their own affairs enables them to put a convincing case. It would have been embarrassing if, after talking to him, I saw my experiences in a different light, and came to believe that the situation in the West Bank was justifiable and not as bad as it had seemed. On the other hand, in sticking to my guns, I could neither be unreasonable nor unwilling to listen. I was sure that whatever the outcome, it would be I and not the press attaché who was likely to lose ground.

I met him in the middle of March 1993, at the Manchester headquarters of the Zionist Central Council. Five of us were present including two of his staff and the secretary of the North-West Friends of Israel Association. He listened to me for half an hour. When I had finished he said, 'You have seen it as it is.' There was no denial. 'If I can be of help in taking up the cases of any of the people you have mentioned then please give me the details. There is one thing you must understand about collective punishment, however. The whole Palestinian community, men, women and children is in a struggle against us. To keep the lid on, we need to use collective punishment. I hope therefore that the peace process will continue until Palestinians have complete autonomy. Perhaps then there can be real peace.'

'Perhaps', I thought, 'but even if autonomy comes,

wounds on both sides of the conflict will not heal without repentance and generous forgiveness.'

Though he accepted what I said, it did not imply that people locally would not be distressed by the stance I had taken. Before I could finally make the decision about resignation, I and a handful of other clergy were invited to the home of Sir Sidney Hamburger, to meet the Israeli Ambassador, Yoav Biran. As Yoav Biran talked about the Palestinian peace process, I wanted to chip in and tell him what I had discovered when in Israel. I thought that if I did so, it would be the final nail. At the end of the talk, I could contain myself no longer. I challenged the Ambassador about collective punishment, in particular curfews and the closure of schools. I cited examples. He expressed surprise that the punishments which I alleged to have happened were as severe as I said they were. If indeed the incidents had happened, he said he would take up the cases. At the end of the meeting, I was urged to send him details of all my findings so that he could investigate them. I explained that I could not give him details without the permission of those involved.

A few days after the meeting, I dictated a letter to Sir Sidney offering my resignation. This was against my emotions but was done to spare the Jewish community further pain and embarrassment. Before the letter was typed, I received a letter from Sir Sidney. He wrote in a gracious and appeasing manner. He said that men of honour should be able to have different views about the same subject without falling out and, said he 'would not support any physical brutality of the type that you mentioned in the meeting with the Ambassador'. Without saying it outright, he plainly wanted me to retain the chairmanship. A telephone call to him confirmed this. I also learnt that the meeting of the Friends of Israel had not been cancelled because of me: there were other practical reasons behind the cancellation.

I went to my dictating machine and wiped out the letter

of resignation. I would have to walk a tightrope, campaigning for Palestinians and retaining the chairmanship of an organisation, many of whose members were right-wing Zionist. It was therefore important to keep Sir Sidney informed of anything that I might be doing to rock the boat.

On the evening of Wednesday 7 July 1993, I pushed a copy of the manuscript of this book through his letter box. The following day, he faxed a dozen pages, mainly the eighth Station, to the Israeli Embassy, in the hope that some of my allegations might be refuted. Their four page reply arrived at his office the following day, Friday. With the onset of the Shabbatt, he was unable to get the document to me until the following night. After telephoning me, he brought it round at 11:15 p.m.

We sat at my desk, comparing my manuscript with the reply from the Embassy. The reply pointed out that while I had reported that the Israelis were suppressing education in the West Bank, the number of students and teachers had doubled since the occupation in 1967. They gave no comparison with the growth in education in Israel, nor did they deny any of my specific allegations I had reported in this area. The reply went on to claim that the overwhelming majority of land used for Jewish settlements is either state land or land owned by Jews. 'Israel does not use private Arab land for settlements.'

I found myself shaking my head as I read the four page document. I might have got my wires crossed on one or two points but I could not deny the bulk of what I had seen and heard. The evidence was too great.

At a quarter past midnight, Sir Sidney and I were no further forward. 'Let me make a deal with you', I said. 'Next year, we'll go to Israel together. For half the time, you take me where you will, and for half the time I'll show you around.' He instantly agreed and we set provisional dates.

When I showed him to the door, we shook hands, our

friendship closer than ever before. As he was going down the steps, I said, 'See you at the next committee meeting.'

'Yes', he replied. 'See you then.' He paused and then with a pensive smile, said slowly, 'Yes, see you then and next year in Jerusalem.'

It is Monday 13 September. I am on a conference at Swanwick in Derbyshire. At 10 o'clock in the evening, I go into the lounge to watch the news. Shimon Peres, the Israeli Foreign Minister, and Mahmoud Abbas, one of Yasser Arafat's closest colleagues, are shown at the White House signing a peace agreement between Israel and the Palestine Liberation Organisation. This is the first move towards giving Palestine self-rule. In front of a large crowd, Yasser Arafat of the PLO and Yitzhak Rabin, the Israeli Prime Minister, shake hands. For many years they fought on opposing sides. Arafat was commander-in-chief of the PLO and Rabin an Israeli general.

Rabin now addresses the onlookers. 'We have come from a land where parents bury their children. We who have fought against you, the Palestinians, we say to you today in a loud, clear voice: Enough of blood and tears, enough . . . The time for peace has come.'

Then Mr Arafat, dressed in chequered keffiyeh and military uniform, replies: 'I assure you that we share your values of freedom, justice and human rights for which my people have been striving. Our two peoples want to give peace a chance.'

The President of the United States, Bill Clinton, then speaks into the microphone. 'This is a bold gamble for peace.'

It is a gamble indeed. The two sides have many issues to resolve, not least agreement on the question of boundaries of the areas to be given self-rule, but also on the future of

East Jerusalem. The negotiations will be made even more difficult by those aiming to torpedo the agreement.

While the signing was taking place, many Israelis were protesting in Jerusalem and calling for Mr Rabin's resignation. Shortly afterwards, Islamic Jihad, anticipating the treaty, killed three Israeli soldiers in the Gaza Strip. A spokesman said, 'It is a gift to Yasser Arafat and all traitors.' He went on to pledge to continue the armed struggle and to kill Arafat himself. The peace agreement is but the first step on the long road towards Palestinian self-rule. The dangers are immense. Both sides need all the help they can get from mutual friends.

Sir Sidney has changed his mind about our proposed trip. 'I have no desire to wear a martyr's crown', he said. The task of building bridges might now be easier, but there is still much work to be done.